Critters
of Wisconsin

Pocket Guide to Animals in Your State

ALEX TROUTMAN

produced in cooperation with
Wildlife Forever

Adventure PUBLICATIONS

an imprint of Adventure**KEEN**

About Wildlife Forever

Wildlife Forever works to conserve America's outdoor heritage through conservation education, preservation of habitat, and scientific management of fish and wildlife. Wildlife Forever is a 501c3 nonprofit organization dedicated to restoring habitat and teaching the next generation about conservation. Become a member and learn more about innovative programs like the Art of Conservation®, The Fish and Songbird Art Contests®, Clean Drain Dry Initiative™, and Prairie City USA®. For more information, visit wildlifeforever.org.

Thank you to Ann McCarthy, the original creator of the Critters series, for her dedication to wildlife conservation and to environmental education. Ann dedicates her work to her daughters, Megan and Katharine Anderson.

Front cover photos by **COULANGES/shutterstock.com:** snowy owl, **James DeBoer/shutterstock.com:** eastern garter snake, **Amy Lutz/shutterstock.com:** bobcat; Back cover photo by **Tom Reichner/Shutterstock.com:** American badger

Edited by Brett Ortler and Jenna Barron
Cover and book design by Jonathan Norberg
Proofreader: Emily Beaumont

10 9 8 7 6 5 4 3 2 1

Critters of Wisconsin
First Edition 2005, Second Edition 2024
Copyright © 2005 by Wildlife Forever, Copyright © 2024 by Alex Troutman
The first edition (2005) of this book was produced by Wildlife Forever.
AdventureKEEN is grateful for its continued partnership and advocacy
on behalf of the natural world.

Published by Adventure Publications
An imprint of AdventureKEEN
310 Garfield Street South, Cambridge, Minnesota 55008
(800) 678-7006
www.adventurepublications.net

Cataloging-in-Publication data is available from the Library of Congress
ISBN 978-1-64755-417-0 (pbk.); 978-1-64755-418-7 (ebook)

Acknowledgments

I want to thank everyone who believed in and supported me over the years a host of friends, family, and teachers. I want to especially thank my mom and my siblings Van, Bre, and TJ.

Dedication

I dedicate this book to my brother Van:
May you continue to enjoy the birds and wildlife in heaven.

This book is for all the kids who have a passion for nature and the outdoors, especially ones who identify as Black, Brown, Indigenous, and People of Color. May this be an encouragement to never give up. And if you have a dream and passion for something, pursue it relentlessly. I also hope to set an example that you can be your full, authentic self!

Lastly, I dedicate this book to all those with ADHD, dyslexia, and all other members of the neurodivergent community. While our quirks make things more challenging, our goals are not impossible to reach; sometimes it takes a little more time and help, but we, too, can succeed!

Contents

Mammals

Birds

Reptiles and Amphibians

Introduction

My passion for nature started when I was young. I was always amazed by the sunlit fiery glow of the red-tailed hawks as they soared overhead when I went fishing with my family. The red-tailed hawk was my spark bird—the bird that captures your attention and gets you into birding. Through my many encounters with red-tailed hawks, and other species like garter snakes and coyotes, I found a passion for nature and the environment. Stumbling across conservationists like Steve Irwin, Jeff Corwin, and Jack Hanna introduced me to the field of Wildlife Biology as a career and gave birth to a dream that I was able to accomplish and live out: serving as a Fish and Wildlife Biologist for governmental agencies, as well as in the private sector.

My childhood dream was driven by a desire to learn more about the different types of ecosystems and the animals that call our wild places home. Books and field guides like this one whet my thirst for knowledge. Even before I could fully understand the words on the pages, I was drawn to books and flashcards that had animals on them. I could identify every animal I was shown and tell a fact about it. I hope that this edition of *Critters of Wisconsin* can be the fuel that sustains your passion for not only learning about wildlife, but also for caring for the environment and making sure that all are welcome in the outdoors. For others, may this book be the spark that ignites a flame for wildlife preservation and environmental stewardship. I hope that this book inspires children from lower socioeconomic and minority backgrounds to pursue their dreams to the fullest and be unapologetically themselves.

By profession, I'm a Fish and Wildlife Biologist, and I'm a nature enthusiast through and through. My love for nature includes making sure that everyone has an equal opportunity to enjoy the outdoors in their own way. So, as you use this book, I encourage you to be intentional in inviting others to enjoy nature with you. Enjoy your discoveries and stay curious!

–Alex Troutman

Wisconsin: The Badger State

Wisconsin is known for its farmlands and livestock, especially the dairy cows that inspire its second nickname: America's Dairyland. Wisconsin was first home to many Indigenous tribes (11 who still live there today), including the Dakota, Ojibwe, Menominee, Ho-Chunk, and Potawatomi. Wisconsin's name is believed to mean something like "a river running through a red place," and the "red" may refer to red sandstone.

Wisconsin is in the midwestern United States and has five geological areas. In the north is Lake Superior and the lowlands. Funnily enough, while Minnesota is called the Land of 10,000 Lakes, Wisconsin has around 15,000! The Northern Highland is next, taking up a third of the state and consisting of many woodlands, lakes, and the state's highest point, Timms Hill. Then there is the Central Plain, which has the red sandstone gorges. Finally, the Eastern Ridges and Lowlands area is where the best farmland is found. It is also where Lake Michigan's beaches and bluffs are.

These environments are home to many animals, including 70-plus species of mammals, more than 400 species of birds, and around 55 species of reptiles and amphibians, not to mention fish, countless insects and spiders, mushrooms, plants, and more. This is your guide to the animals, birds, reptiles, and amphibians that call Wisconsin home.

Some of Wisconsin's most iconic plants, animals, and other natural resources are now officially recognized as state symbols. Get to know them below and see if you can spot them all! You'll probably encounter the state nickname and motto, so I've included them here too.

State Bird:
American robin

State Fruit:
cranberry

State Tree:
sugar maple

State Flower:
wood violet

State Fish:
muskellunge

State Fossil:
trilobite

State Animal:
American badger

State Insect:
honeybee

State Nickname:
The Badger
State/
America's
Dairyland

State Motto:
Forward

How to Use This Guide

This book is your introduction to some of the wonderful critters found in Wisconsin; it includes 23 mammals, 31 birds, and 11 reptiles and amphibians. It includes some animals you probably already know, such as deer and bald eagles, but others you may not know about, such as eastern massasauga rattlesnakes or rose-breasted grosbeaks. I've selected the species in this book because they are widespread (American badger, page 12), abundant (black-capped chickadee, page 68), or well-known but best observed from a safe distance (black bear, page 16).

The book is organized by type of animals: mammals, birds, and reptiles and amphibians. Within each section, the animals are in alphabetical order. If you'd like to look for a critter quickly, turn to the checklist (page 140), which you can also use to keep track of how many animals you've seen! For each species, you'll see a photo of the animal, along with neat facts and information on the animal's habitat, diet, its predators, how it raises its young, and more.

Safety Note

Nature can be unpredictable, so don't go outdoors alone, and always tell an adult when you're going outside. All wild animals should be treated with respect. If you see one—big or small—don't get close to it or attempt to touch or feed it. Instead, keep your distance and enjoy spotting it. If you can, snap some pictures with a camera or make a quick drawing using a sketchbook. If the animal is getting too close, is acting strangely, or seems sick or injured, tell an adult right away, as it might have rabies, a disease that can affect mammals. The good news is there's a rabies vaccine, so it's important to visit a doctor right away if you get bit or scratched by a wild animal.

Notes About Icons

Each species page includes basic information about each animal, from what it eats to how it survives the winter. The book also includes information that's neat to know; in the mammals section, each page includes a simple track illustration of each animal, with approximate track size included. And along the bottom, there is an example track pattern for each mammal, with the exception for those that primarily glide or fly (flying squirrels and bats).

On the left-hand page for each mammal, a rough-size illustration is included that shows how big each animal is compared to a basketball.

Also on the left-hand page, there are icons that tell you when each animal is most active: nocturnal (at night), diurnal (during the day), or crepuscular (at dawn/dusk), so you know when to look. If an animal has a "zzz" icon, it hibernates during the winter. Some animals hibernate every winter, and their internal processes (breathing and heartbeat) slow down almost entirely. Other animals only partially hibernate, but this still helps them save energy and survive through the coldest part of the year.

nocturnal
(active at night)

diurnal
(active during day)

crepuscular
(most active at
dawn and dusk)

hibernates/deep sleeper
(dormant during winter)

ground nest cup nest platform nest cavity nest migrates

On the left-hand side of each bird page, the nest for each species is shown, along with information on whether or not the bird migrates; on the right-hand side, there's information on where it goes.

Did you know?

Badgers are solitary animals, but they will sometimes hunt with coyotes in a team. A coyote will chase prey into the badger's den, and the badger will chase or dig out the prey that coyotes like. The badger's den has one entrance with a pile of dirt next to it. When a badger is threatened, it will back into its burrow and show its teeth.

Size Comparison   Most Active   Track Size 2¾"   Hibernates

American Badger

Taxidea taxus

Size: 2–3 feet long; weighs 8–25 pounds

Habitat: Savannas, grasslands, and meadows

Range: Can be found throughout Wisconsin and westward through the Great Plains to the West Coast and southward to Mexico

Food: Carnivores; they eat pocket gophers, moles, ground squirrels, and other rodents. They will also eat dead animals (or carrion), fish, reptiles, and a few types of birds, especially ground-nesting birds.

Den: Badgers are fossorial (a digging animal that spends a lot of time underground); they build many dens or burrows throughout their range. Most dens are used to store food, but badgers also use dens to sleep in and raise their young. Dens can be over 10 feet deep and 4 feet wide.

Young: Cubs are born, with eyes closed, usually in April or May in litters of 2–3. Extensive care is provided by the mom for up to 3 months. After another 2–3 months, the young will gain their independence.

Predators: Bears, bobcats, cougars, coyotes, gray wolves, golden eagles, and humans

Tracks: The front tracks are 2¾ inches long and 2 inches wide.

The American badger is a short, bulky mammal with grayish to dirty-red fur. Badgers have a distinctive face with a series of cream-and-white stripes offset by a black background.

Did you know?

Beavers are rodents! Yes, these flat-tailed mammals are rodents, like rats and squirrels. In fact, they are the largest native rodents in North America. Just like other rodents, beavers have large incisors, which they use to chew through trees to build dams and dens. Beavers are the original wetland engineers. By damming rivers and streams, beavers create ponds and wetlands.

Size Comparison   Most Active   Track Size

American Beaver

Castor canadensis

Size: Body is 25–30 inches long; tail is 9–13 inches long; weighs 30–70 pounds

Habitat: Wooded wetland areas near ponds, streams, and lakes

Range: Beavers can be found throughout Wisconsin and in much of the rest of the United States.

Food: Leaves, twigs, and stems; they also feed on fruits and aquatic plant roots; throughout the year they gather and store tree cuttings, which they eat in winter.

Den: A beaver's home is called a lodge. It consists of a pile of branches that is splattered with mud and vegetation. Lodges are constructed on the banks of lakes and streams and have exits and entrances that are underwater.

Young: Young beavers (kits) are born in late April through May and June in litters of 3–4. After two years they are considered mature and will be forced out of the den.

Predators: Bobcats, cougars, bears, wolves, and coyotes. Human trappers are major predators too.

Tracks: A beaver's front foot looks a lot like your hand; it has five fingers. The hind (back) foot is long, with five separate toes that have webbing or extra skin between them.

Ranges from dark brown to reddish brown. They have a stocky body with hind legs that are longer than the front legs. Their body is covered in dense fur, but the tail is naked. A beaver's tail has special blood vessels that help it cool or warm its body.

15

Did you know?

Female bears weigh between 90 and 300 pounds and are smaller than the average adult human male in the US. But don't let their small size fool you; with a bite force around 800 pounds per square inch (PSI) and a swiping force of over 400 pounds, these bears are not to be taken lightly.

Size Comparison Most Active Track Size 6–7" Hibernates

Black Bear

Ursus americanus

Size: 5–6 feet long (nose to tail); weighs 90–600 pounds

Habitat: Forests, lowland areas, and swamps

Range: In Wisconsin, black bears can be found throughout the northern parts of the state. They can be found in many parts of North America, from Alaska down through Canada and into Mexico.

Food: Berries, fish, seeded crops, small mammals, wild grapes, tree shoots, ants, bees, beavers, and even deer fawns

Den: Denning usually starts in December, with bears emerging in late March or April. Dens can be either dug (out of a hillside, for example) or constructed with materials such as leaves, grass, and moss.

Young: Two cubs are usually born at one time (a litter), often in January. Cubs are born blind and without fur, with pink skin. They weigh 8–16 ounces.

Predators: Humans and other bears. Sometimes, other carnivores, such as mountain lions, wolves, coyotes, or even bobcats, will prey on black bears. Cubs are especially vulnerable.

Tracks: Front print is usually 4–6 inches long and 3½–5 inches wide, with the hind foot being 6–7 inches long and 3½–5 inches wide. The feet have five toes.

Black bears are usually black in color, but they can be many different variations of black and brown. Some even have grayish, reddish, or blond fur.

Did you know?
Bobcats get their name from their short tail; a "bob" is a type of short haircut. They have the largest range of all wild cats in the United States. Bobcats can even hunt prey much larger than themselves; in fact, they can take down prey that is over four times their size, such as white-tailed deer!

Size Comparison Most Active Track Size

Bobcat

Lynx rufus

Size: 27–48 inches head to tail; males weigh around 30 pounds, while females weigh 24 pounds or so.

Habitat: Dense forests, scrub areas (forests of low trees and bushes), swamps, and even some urban (city) areas

Range: In Wisconsin, they have been found throughout the state; they are widespread throughout the United States.

Food: Squirrels, birds, rabbits and snowshoe hares, and white-tailed deer fawns; occasionally even adult deer and porcupines!

Den: Dense shrubs, caves, or even hollow trees; dens can be lined with leaves or moss.

Young: Bobcats usually breed in early winter through spring. Females give birth to a litter of 2–4 kittens. Bobcats become independent around 7–8 months, and they reach reproductive maturity at 1 year for females and at 2 years for males.

Predators: Occasionally fishers and coyotes; humans also hunt and trap bobcats for fur.

Tracks: Roughly 2 inches wide; both front and back paws have four toe pads and a carpal pad (a pad below the toe pads).

Bobcats have a white belly and a brown or pale-gray top with black spots. The tail usually has a black tip. They are mostly crepuscular (say it, cre-pus-cue-lar), which means they are most active in the dawn and twilight hours.

Did you know?

At one time, coyotes were only found in the central and western parts of the US, but now, with the help of humans (eliminating predators and clearing forests), they can be found throughout most of the country. Coyotes can jump over 3 meters horizontally.

Size Comparison   Most Active   Track Size

Coyote

Canis latrans

Size: 3–4 feet long; weighs 21–50 pounds

Habitat: Urban and suburban areas, woodlands, grasslands, and farm fields

Range: Coyotes can be found in all the counties of Wisconsin. They are also found throughout the US and Mexico, the northern parts of Central America, and in southern Canada.

Food: A variety of prey, including rodents, birds, deer, and sometimes livestock

Den: Coyotes will dig their own dens but will often use old fox or badger dens or hollow logs.

Young: 5–7 pups, independent around 8–10 months

Predators: Bears and wolves; humans trap and kill for pelts and to "protect" livestock.

Tracks: Four toes and a carpal pad (the single pad below the toe pads) can be seen on all four feet.

Coyotes have brown, reddish-brown, or gray back fur with a lighter gray-to-white belly. They have a longer muzzle than other wild canines. They are active mostly during the night (nocturnal) but also during the twilight and dawn hours (crepuscular).

Did you know?

The eastern cottontail gets its name from its short, puffy tail that looks like a cotton ball. A cottontail can travel up to 18 miles per hour! Rabbits have great hearing and eyesight. They can almost see all the way around them (360 degrees). On days with high wind, they will bed down in a burrow because the wind interferes with their ability to hear and detect predators.

Size Comparison   Most Active   Track Size

Eastern Cottontail

Sylvilagus floridanus

Size: 16–19 inches long; weighs 1½–4 pounds

Habitat: Forests, swamps, orchards, deserts, and farm areas

Range: Found throughout Wisconsin; throughout the eastern US to Arizona and New Mexico; isolated ranges in the Pacific Northwest

Food: Clovers; grasses; wild strawberries; garden plants; and twigs of a variety of trees, including maple, oak, and sumac

Den: Rabbits don't dig dens; they bed in shallow, grassy, saucer-shaped depressions (holes) or under shrubs. They will sometimes use woodchuck dens in the winter.

Young: They usually have 2–4 kits at one time, but it's not uncommon to have 7 or more. Born naked and blind, they weigh about an ounce (about the same weight as a slice of bread) and gain weight very quickly.

Predators: Owls, coyotes, eagles, weasels, humans, and foxes

Tracks: The front foot is an inch long with four toe pads; the hind foot is 3½ inches long.

An eastern cottontail sports thick brown fur with a white belly, a gray rump, and a white "cotton" tail. During the winter, it survives by eating bark off of fruit trees and shrubs.

Did you know?

The eastern fox squirrel's bones appear pink under ultraviolet (UV) light, a type of light human eyes can't see. Squirrels accidentally help plant trees by forgetting where they have previously buried nuts. Sometimes, they seem to pretend to bury nuts to throw off would-be nut thieves.

Size Comparison   Most Active   Track Size

2½"

Eastern Fox Squirrel

Sciurus niger

Size: 19–28 inches long; weighs 1–3 pounds

Habitat: Open woodlands, suburban areas, and dense forest

Range: They are found throughout much of Wisconsin except the northwestern parts of the state; throughout the eastern United States to Texas and as far north as the Dakotas.

Food: Acorns, seeds, nuts, insects such as moths and beetles, birds, eggs, and dead fish

Den: Ball-shaped dreys, or nests, are made of vegetation like leaves, sometimes in tree cavities.

Young: 2–3 kits are born between late January to April and late June through August. Kittens are born naked and weigh half an ounce; they are cared for by their parents for the first 7–8 weeks. They can reproduce by around 10–11 months for males and 8 months for females.

Predators: Humans, hawks, cats, coyotes, bobcats, and weasels

Tracks: The front tracks have four digits (toes), and the hind feet have five digits.

The eastern fox squirrel is the largest tree squirrel in Wisconsin. It is gray or reddish brown with a yellowish or light-brown underside. There is also a black and smoky-gray color phase. Both the male and female look the same.

Did you know?

Elk are known to be the loudest of all cervids (deer family). Males produce a low-pitched bellow or roar, called a bugle. Bugling is a technique that involves both roaring and whistling at the same time. Elk use their bugle or bugling to attract mates or announce territories during the fall mating season. Their bugles can be heard over long distances.

Size Comparison

Most Active

Track Size
4½"

Elk

Cervus elaphus canadensis

Size: 5–8 feet tall; weighs 377–1,095 pounds

Habitat: Open woodlands, mountain areas, shrublands, coniferous swamps, and hardwood forests

Range: Found in small areas in northwestern and central parts of Wisconsin. They are found in the western US with isolated populations in eastern states.

Food: Elk are herbivores that eat grasses; flowers; and leaves from trees like cedar, red maple, and basswood.

Den: No den; will lay in grass to rest. Mother elk will hide young calves in tall grasses.

Young: Calves are born after 240–265 days. At birth, calves weigh around 30 pounds and have spots through the first summer. Separation from mother's milk happens around the 60 day mark, but calves will continue to get care and protection from mom for around a year. They reach full maturity around 16 months, but males will usually wait to mate until they are older.

Predators: Cougars or mountain lions, gray wolves, and bears. Calves may fall victim to bobcats and coyotes.

Tracks: Front tracks of an adult are about 4¾ inches long and wide. Hind foot tracks are 4½ inches long and 3½ inches wide. Two toes are on both feet.

Elk come in different shades of browns and tans. In the summer and spring they are lighter brown to tan, while in the winter they are a deep dark brown; during both seasons, they have a cream or off-white rump. They sport a darker tone on the head, neck, belly, and legs.

Did you know?

While named fishers, they do not catch fish. They are sometimes called fisher cats, but they are not related to cats. Instead, they eat fruits, berries, mammals, bugs, and other critters.

Size Comparison   Most Active   Track Size

Fisher

Pekania pennanti

Size: 29–47 inches long; weighs 4–13 pounds

Habitat: Forests

Range: Fishers are found in most of northern Wisconsin, with isolated sightings in the central parts of the state; they can be found throughout the northeastern states of the US, into Canada and as far north as Alaska, and down the Pacific Coast into California.

Food: Omnivores that feed on berries, birds, reptiles, eggs, insects, and mammals

Den: Hollow trees or bushes

Young: Usually 1–4 kits are born per litter. Young are born with eyes closed; at around 7 weeks, they will open their eyes, and 1–2 weeks later they will begin to eat solid food. They are forced out of the den at around 5 months old and reach reproductive maturity around 1 year for females and 2 years for males.

Predators: Bears, eagles, coyotes, owls, lynx, and mountain lions

Tracks: Front tracks have five toes with claws; they're 2–4 inches long (same for the back length) and 2½–4 inches wide with a visible paw pad. Hind tracks are 2–3 inches wide; back paw pad is covered with fur.

Fishers are a medium-size member of the weasel family. They are a long-bodied animal that is stout or low to the ground. Their fur is deep brown to black. Fur of the face and chest areas can be golden brown to dirty blond.

Did you know?

All wolves in the United States (except the red wolf in the Southeast) are gray wolves! Each area has its own subspecies (a group that is a little different physically or genetically), and their common names are often based on their habitat. Gray wolves are often referred to as timber wolves. In Wisconsin and the eastern US, gray wolves will travel over 12 miles a night during fall and winter.

Size Comparison   Most Active   Track Size

4"

Gray Wolf

Canis lupus

Size: 5–6½ feet long; weighs 60–130 pounds

Habitat: Forests and grasslands

Range: They are found throughout central and northern Wisconsin. They can be found throughout much of Canada and Alaska, as well as many states out west and in a few states of northern New England.

Food: Deer; moose; elk; and smaller animals like rabbits, beavers, and birds. Sometimes wolves feed young (or pups) vegetation, such as blueberries.

Den: For the first couple of weeks, the female stays with the pups to keep them warm and fed. During this time, she is totally dependent on the remainder of the pack to provide her with food. Once the pups are large enough to be alone, the female can leave them and hunt to support the growing pack.

Young: Pups are born in April or May; 4 to 7 pups are born at one time; they stay in the den for 6–8 weeks and eventually leave the pack at 1–2 years of age.

Predators: Bears, other wolves, coyotes (which prey on young wolves), and humans

Tracks: Front paws are around 5 inches long; hind paws are 4 inches long; both front and hind paws have a width of 3–3½ inches.

Gray wolves can be gray, black, or even red. Wolves live in groups called packs. Packs can be as small as 2 wolves and as large as 13 or more. Wolves will hunt in packs; when hunts are successful, the whole pack will feed on the kill.

Did you know?

Bats are the only mammals that can really fly. All other "flying" mammals use extra skin to glide through the air, while bats can use their wings to achieve lift, just like birds!

Size Comparison   Most Active   Hibernates

Little Brown Bat

Myotis lucifugus

Size: 3–4½ inches long; wingspan of 8–9 inches; weighs less than an ounce

Habitat: Wooded areas, caves, and suburban areas

Range: They are found throughout Wisconsin but are most common in the southeastern and western parts of the state; also found throughout the United States and northern Mexico.

Food: Flying insects like moths, beetles, and mosquitoes

Den: Bats den in groups called colonies; roosting sites are in hollow trees, caves, and even buildings. Bats roost in groups called maternity colonies, which are made up of females and pups.

Young: Females give birth to one pup, which will hang onto its mother; pups begin flying at 3 weeks.

Predators: Owls, snakes, raccoons, and outdoor cats

Tracks: Bats don't often leave tracks, but you can smell and see bat droppings (guano) in roosting sites.

The little brown bat is a short-eared bat with dark-brown ears and snout; each fall, when temperatures drop, bats migrate to their favorite hibernation sites such as caves, tunnels, and wells. If you see a bat, don't touch it, but tell an adult; bats usually keep to themselves, so a bat spotted near people may be sick. Bats can sometimes be spotted outside, and those are often perfectly healthy.

The little brown bat does not often leave tracks.

Did you know?
The meadow vole is the largest vole that is found in Wisconsin.
When threatened, voles will stomp their hind feet like a rabbit
does. A meadow vole can eat over 50% of its body weight per day.

Size Comparison   Most Active   Track Size

Meadow Vole

Microtus pennsylvanicus

Size: 5–7 inches long; weighs 1–2½ ounces

Habitat: Grasslands, swamps, meadows, marshes, woodlands, farmlands, and open woody areas

Range: They are found throughout Wisconsin, the northern US, and Canada.

Food: Seeds, grasses, fruit, leaves, and sedges (marsh plants)

Den: No dens; they will nest aboveground or in a shallow nest at or just below the ground.

Young: 4–6 offspring per litter; young are born blind and without fur. Female cares for young for 2 weeks; young reach reproductive maturity at around 5–6 weeks.

Predators: Owls, hawks, snakes, weasels, foxes, and cats

Tracks: The front foot is smaller than the hind foot and has four toes, the hind foot is larger with five toes.

The meadow vole has dark-brown fur on the back with a white-to-silver underbelly. It has small ears and black eyes. Voles create tracks or runways in grass and snow. Voles help the environment by turning over the soil when they dig, and their waste provides nutrients to the soil.

Did you know?

Mink have webbed feet, like otters. Although they usually dive and swim short distances, mink can dive over 13 feet deep and swim for over 95 feet underwater, if necessary!

Size Comparison   Most Active   Track Size

1¾"

Mink

Mustela vison

Size: 16–27 inches long; weighs 1½–3½ pounds

Habitat: Wetland areas with dense vegetation near streams, lakes, and swamps

Range: They are found across much of Wisconsin, as well as throughout most of the US and Canada.

Food: Fish, eggs, snakes, muskrats, farm animals, small mammals, and aquatic animals such as crayfish

Den: Their dens are near water, in holes in the ground, hollow logs, and old muskrat and beaver lodges; they will use grass or fur from prey as bedding.

Young: At birth, they weigh less than an ounce; mothers give birth to 3–6 young, called kits. They are mature at 1 year old.

Predators: Otters, birds of prey, wolves, coyotes, bobcats, internal parasites, and humans (who trap them for fur)

Tracks: Both the front and hind tracks resemble a gloved hand. Both the left and right tracks are seen parallel to each other because the mink often bound (leap) when moving. Tracks are usually seen near water.

A mostly nocturnal (active at night) animal, it has a shiny or glossy dark-brown coat that it keeps all year long. Mink usually have a white or pale-yellow chest patch or bib on the throat that sometimes extends to the belly.

Did you know?

Moose belong to the deer family, and they are the largest members of the deer family in the world! They can rotate their ears 180 degrees. Moose can swim over 5 miles per hour for over 8 miles, and they can also run over 35 miles per hour. Moose will dive beneath the water of ponds and lakes to reach the plants at the bottom.

Size Comparison   Most Active   Track Size

Moose

Alces alces

Size: 7–10 feet long; 5–6½ feet from the shoulder to the ground; weighs 750–1,200 pounds or more

Habitat: Forested areas, marshes, wetlands, and swamps

Range: They can be found in northern Wisconsin along the areas that border Minnesota and the upper peninsula of Michigan, as well as in Canada, Alaska, and the northern parts of the eastern US. There are populations in Wyoming, Colorado, and a number of western states.

Food: Leaves, bark, twigs, roots, and aquatic plants

Den: Like other deer, moose dig out beds amid the forest floor.

Young: 1–2 young (calves) that are 25–35 pounds at birth; moose are considered adults at around 2 years old.

Predators: Bears, wolves, and humans

Tracks: Hoofprints are large and heart-shaped.

Moose are a deep brown with a hump on the shoulder and a dewlap (a flap of skin, which is also known as a "bell") hanging down from the throat area. Males are larger than females, and they have large, flat antlers that can be over 4 feet wide and weigh over 30 pounds.

Did you know?

A single porcupine can have over 30,000 quills that it can use to protect itself from predators. Porcupine quills are hollow and can be over 2 inches long. Porcupines are herbivores (plant eaters), and they have a special bacteria in their digestive system to help them break down the plant material.

Size Comparison   Most Active   Track Size

3⅜"

North American Porcupine

Erethizon dorsatum

Size: 2–3 feet long; weighs 10–25 pounds

Habitat: Forested areas, grasslands, and deserts

Range: They are found throughout northern parts of the state; they are also found throughout Canada and various areas across the northern and western US.

Food: Skunk cabbage, clovers, twigs, leaves, and tree bark

Den: They den in hollow logs and tree cavities.

Young: One young (porcupette) is born between May and July; they weigh a pound at birth and have 1-inch quills.

Predators: Lynx, bobcats, coyotes, owls, and fishers

Tracks: The front foot is shorter than the hind foot; the hind foot has five toes, while the front only has four toes.

The North American porcupine is mostly nocturnal; its fur is black to gray and shades of brown with obvious quills. When threatened, it will turn around and strike an attacker with its tail quills, which are 4 inches long and are like needles. With that many quills, porcupines sometimes accidentally poke themselves. To protect itself (from itself), the porcupine has a special substance on its quills that acts like an antibiotic (or medicine). This prevents it from getting infected after an accidental poke. Like other mammals, porcupines need salt and will chew on, or lick, objects with the mineral to fulfill that craving. Sometimes this leads to porcupines chewing on human-made structures.

Did you know?

The raccoon is great at catching fish and other aquatic animals, such as mussels and crayfish. They are also excellent swimmers, but they apparently avoid swimming because the water makes their fur heavy. Raccoons can turn their feet 180 degrees; this helps them when climbing, especially when going headfirst down trees.

Size Comparison   Most Active   Track Size 3"   Hibernates

Northern Raccoon

Procyon lotor

Size: 24–40 inches long; weighs 15–28 pounds

Habitat: Woody areas, grasslands, suburban and urban areas, wetlands, and marshes

Range: They are found throughout Wisconsin and the US; they are also found in Mexico and southern Canada.

Food: Eggs, insects, garbage, garden plants, berries, nuts, fish, carrion, small mammals, and aquatic invertebrates like crayfish and mussels

Den: Raccoon dens are built in hollow trees, abandoned burrows, caves, and human-made structures.

Young: 2–6 young (kits) are born around March through July. They are born weighing 2 ounces, are around 4 inches long, and are blind with lightly colored fur.

Predators: Coyotes, foxes, bobcats, humans, and even large birds of prey

Tracks: Their front tracks resemble human handprints. The back tracks sort of look like human footprints.

The northern raccoon has dense fur with variations of brown, black, and white streaks. It has black, mask-like markings on its face and a black-and-gray/brownish ringed tail. During the fall, it will grow a thick layer of fat to stay warm in the winter.

Did you know?

Otters are good swimmers and can close their nostrils while diving. This allows them to dive for as long as 8 minutes and to depths of over 50 feet. Otter fur is the thickest of all mammal fur. River otters have an incredible 67,000 hairs for every square centimeter!

Size Comparison

Most Active

Track Size

3"

Northern River Otter

Lontra canadensis

Size: 29–48 inches long; weighs 10–33 pounds

Habitat: Lakes, marshes, rivers, and large streams; suburban areas

Range: Otters can be found throughout Wisconsin; they are found across much of the US, except parts of the Southwest and portions of the central US.

Food: Fish, frogs, snakes, crabs, crayfish, mussels, birds, eggs, turtles, and small mammals. They sometimes eat aquatic vegetation too.

Den: They den in burrows along the river, usually under rocks, riverbanks, hollow trees, and vegetation.

Young: 2–4 young (pups) are born between November and May. Pups are born with their eyes closed. They will leave the area at around 6 months old and reach full maturity at around 2 or 3 years.

Predators: Coyotes, bobcats, bears, and dogs

Tracks: Their feet have nonretractable claws and are webbed.

Northern river otters have thick, dark-brown fur with a long, slender body. Their fur is made up of two types: a short undercoat and a coarse top coat that repels water. They have webbed feet and a layer of fat that helps keep them warm in cold water.

Did you know?

The red fox is a great jumper and can leap over 13 feet in one bound. Red foxes are also fast, as they can run up to 30 miles per hour. Red foxes, like wild cats, will hide their food to eat later, often under leaf litter or in holes.

Size Comparison   Most Active   Track Size

2¼"

Red Fox

Vulpes vulpes

Size: 37–42 inches long; weighs 8–15 pounds

Habitat: Grasslands, forest edges, farm fields, and suburban areas

Range: Foxes are common throughout much of the state; they can be found in nearly all of the US, except for the Southwest.

Food: They are omnivores that eat frogs, birds, snakes, small mammals, insects, seeds, nuts, and fruit.

Den: They dig underground dens, sometimes several at once, splitting a litter (babies) between the two. They also use old badger or groundhog holes or tree roots for den sites.

Young: 3–7 young (kits) are born; pups will nurse (drink milk from the mother) for around 10 weeks and will become independent at around 7 months.

Predators: Coyotes, lynx, cougars, and other species of carnivores. Humans trap and hunt foxes for fur.

Tracks: Their footprints resemble dog tracks and have four toe pads; they walk in a line with the hind foot behind the front.

The red fox is a medium-size predator with a burnt orange or rust-like red coat with a bushy, white-tipped tail. The legs are usually black or grayish. The red fox's tail is about one third of its body length.

Did you know?

Snowshoe hares can run over 30 miles per hour and can jump over 12 feet in a single leap. Their name comes from their hind feet, which are large and furry and look (and act) like snowshoes.

Size Comparison

Most Active

Track Size

4–5"

Snowshoe Hare

Lepus americanus

Size: 17–22 inches long; tail is 2 inches long; weighs 3–4½ pounds

Habitat: Woody areas, swamps, open fields, and forest bogs

Range: They are found throughout much of the northern-most central parts of Wisconsin, the northern US into the Appalachian Mountains, and on the Pacific Coast.

Food: Grasses, flowers, bark, twigs, evergreen needles; they sometimes will eat the remains of other snowshoe hares.

Den: None

Young: They give birth to 2–4 young (known as leverets); during the day, young will hide in different places and will only come together with the mother to nurse (drink milk) for a few short minutes. Young are mature one year after birth.

Predators: Bobcats, coyotes, mink, foxes, and owls and other birds of prey

Tracks: Their hind feet are larger than the front.

The snowshoe hare is a medium-size, rabbit-like animal with brown fur in the summer and a white coat in the winter. They are mostly active during the dawn and dusk hours of the day (crepuscular).

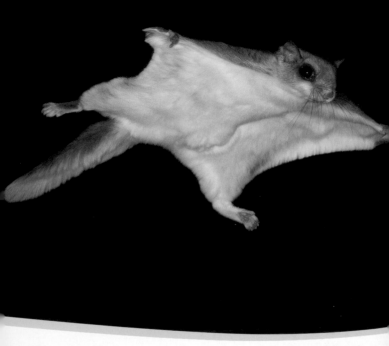

Did you know?
The southern flying squirrel doesn't actually fly! Instead, it uses special folds of skin to glide through the air. They can glide over 100 feet at a time. They have thick paws that aid them in landing. Because they move from tree to tree, they help to spread seeds and fungi.

Size Comparison   Most Active

Southern Flying Squirrel

Glaucomys volans

Size: 9 inches long; weighs 2–3 ounces

Habitat: Forests with older trees

Range: In Wisconsin, they are found throughout much of central and southern parts of the state; throughout the eastern US and parts of Mexico.

Food: Nuts, berries, acorns, small birds, mice, insects, and mushrooms

Den: They make nests in tree hollows. They will also use abandoned woodpecker holes and human-made nest boxes or birdhouses. They line the nest with chewed bark, grasses, moss, and feathers.

Young: 2–3 young (kits) are born per litter; they drink milk from the mother for around 70 days and will be fully independent around 4 months and mature at around a year old.

Predators: Small hawks, foxes, owls, martens (weasel-like mammals), and weasels

Tracks: Tracks are rare because they spend most of their time in trees.

The southern flying squirrel is a grayish-brown nocturnal (active at night) animal that glides through the air from tree to tree. The patagium, or skin fold, stretches from their ankles to their wrist, allowing them to "fly." (People have even built similar "squirrel suits" to glide with, and they've worked!) During winter months, flying squirrels share cavities with others.

The southern flying squirrel does not often leave tracks.

Did you know?

Skunks help farmers! They save farmers money by feeding on rodents and insects that destroy crops. When skunks spray, they can aim really well! When threatened, a skunk will aim its tail towards the threat and spray a stinky musk into the target's face or eyes.

Size Comparison   Most Active   Track Size   Hibernates

1½"

Striped Skunk

Mephitis mephitis

Size: 17–30 inches long; weighs 6–13 pounds

Habitat: Woodlands, prairies, and suburban areas

Range: Found throughout much of Wisconsin; they can be found throughout the US and into Canada and the northern parts of Mexico.

Food: Omnivores (eaters of meat and plants), they eat eggs, fruits, nuts, small mammals, carrion (dead things), insects, amphibians, small reptiles, and even garbage.

Den: Skunks prefer short and shallow natural dens, or dens abandoned by other animals, but will dig dens 3–6 feet long and up to 3 feet deep underground. Dens have multiple hidden entrances, and rooms are usually lined with vegetation.

Young: They have 4–5 young (kits) that are blind at birth; at around 3 weeks they gain vision and the ability to spray.

Predators: Raptors and large carnivores

Tracks: Their front feet have five long, curved claws used for digging; the hind foot also has five toes and is longer and skinnier than the front foot.

The striped skunk is a cat-size, nocturnal (active at night) mammal with black fur and two white stripes that run the entire length of the body. The stripe pattern is usually distinctive to each skunk.

Did you know?

The opossum is the only marsupial native to the US. Marsupials are a special group of animals that are most well-known for their pouches, which they use to carry their young. When frightened, young opossums will play dead (called playing possum) and adults will show their teeth and hiss or run away.

Size Comparison   Most Active   Track Size
2½"

Virginia Opossum

Didelphis virginiana

Size: 22–45 inches long; weighs 4–8 pounds

Habitat: Forests, woodlands, meadows, and suburban areas

Range: They are found throughout Wisconsin, except the most northeastern parts of the state; they are found throughout the eastern US, Canada, and also in Mexico and Costa Rica.

Food: Eggs, small mammals, garbage, insects, worms, birds, fruit, and occasionally small reptiles and amphibians

Den: They den in hollow trees, abandoned animal burrows, and buildings.

Young: A litter of 6–20 young (joeys) are born blind and without fur; their limbs are not fully formed. Young will climb from the birthing area into the mother's pouch and stay until 8 weeks old; they then alternate between the mother's pouch and her back for 4 weeks. At 12 weeks they are independent.

Predators: Hawks, owls, pet cats and dogs, coyotes, and bobcats

Tracks: The front feet are 2 inches long and around 1½ inches wide and resemble a child's hands; the hind feet are 2½ inches long and around 2¼ inches wide; they have fingers in front with a fifth finger that acts as a thumb.

The Virginia opossum has long gray-and-black fur; the face is white, and the tail is pink to gray and furless. Opossums have long claws.

Did you know?

When they first emerge, a deer's antlers are covered in a special skin called velvet. Deer can run up to 40 miles per hour and can jump over 8 feet vertically (high) and over 15 feet horizontally (long).

Size Comparison   Most Active   Track Size

3"

White-tailed Deer

Odocoileus virginianus

Size: 4-6 feet long; 3–4 feet tall at front shoulder; weighs 114–308 pounds

Habitat: Forest edges, brushy fields, woody farmlands, prairies, and swamps

Range: They are found throughout Wisconsin and throughout the US, except for much of the Southwest; they are also found in southern Canada and into South America.

Food: Fruits, grasses, tree shrubs, nuts, and bark

Den: Deer do not den but will bed down in tall grasses and shrubby areas.

Young: Deer usually give birth to twins (fawns) that are 3–6 pounds in late May to June. The fawns are born with spots; this coloration helps them hide in vegetation. Young become independent at 1–2 years.

Predators: Wolves, coyotes, bears, bobcats, and humans

Tracks: Both front and hind feet have two teardrop- or comma-shaped toes.

Crepuscular (active at dawn and dusk), white-tailed deer have big brown eyes with eye rings and a long snout with a black, glossy nose. The males have antlers, which fall off each year. All deer have a white tail that they flash upward when alarmed. Deer molt or change fur color twice a year. They sport a rusty-brown fur in the summer; in early fall, they transition to winter coats that are grayish brown in color.

Did you know?
The American goldfinch helps restore habitats by spreading
seeds. The goldfinch gets its color from a pigment called a
carotenoid (say it, cuh-rot-en-oid) in the seeds it eats. It can even
feed upside down by using its feet to bring seeds to its mouth.

Nest Type   Most Active

American Goldfinch

Spinus tristis

Size: 4½–5 inches long; wingspan of 9 inches; weighs about half an ounce

Habitat: Grasslands, meadows, suburban areas, and wetlands

Range: Found throughout Wisconsin year-round; they can be found throughout much of the United States and southern Canada during various times of the year.

Food: Seeds of plants and trees; sometimes feeds on insects; loves thistle seeds at birdfeeders

Nesting: Goldfinches build a nest in late June.

Nest: Cup-shaped nests are built a couple of feet above-ground out of roots and plant fibers.

Eggs: 2–7 eggs with a bluish-white tint

Young: Young (chicks) hatch around 15 days after being laid; they hatch without feathers and weigh only a gram. Chicks learn to fly after around 11–15 days. Young become mature at around 11 months old.

Predators: Garter snakes, blue jays, American kestrels, and cats

Migration: Nonmigratory in Wisconsin; in some states, it will migrate north for breeding territories and south for wintering areas.

During the summer, American goldfinch males are brightly colored with golden-yellow feathers and an orange beak. They have black wings with white wing bars. The crown (top) of the head is black. In winter, they molt, and the males look more like the females. Females are always greenish yellow with hints of yellow around the head.

Did you know?

American robins have a great sense of hearing. They hunt for earthworms underground using only their hearing. Robins are opportunistic feeders in urban (city) areas; they will wait for lawns to be disturbed by mowers, sprinklers, or rain, and then feed on the worms that have emerged. The American robin is the state bird of Wisconsin!

Nest Type   Most Active   Migrates

American Robin

Turdus migratorius

Size: 9–11 inches long; wingspan of 17 inches; weighs 2½–3 ounces

Habitat: Cities, forests, and lawns

Range: They can be found throughout most of Wisconsin year-round, and during the breeding season they can be found in the far northern parts of the state and throughout North America except the extreme north of Canada.

Food: Fruits, earthworms, beetle grubs, caterpillars, insects, and grasshoppers

Nesting: April to August

Nest: Cup-shaped nests are exclusively built by the female 5–14 feet off the ground in bushes or trees. Nests are constructed of grass, paper, twigs, and feathers. A new nest is built for each set of eggs.

Eggs: 3–5 sky-blue eggs

Young: Eggs hatch after 14 days of incubation; chicks hatch blind and mostly without feathers. Hatchlings (chicks) leave the nest after 2 weeks but will continue to beg for food from parents.

Predators: Snakes, crows, cats, foxes, raccoons, squirrels, raptors, and weasels

Migration: Some birds stay throughout the winter, but the majority (especially in northern Wisconsin) migrate south to warmer areas.

American robin males have a dark black-to-gray head with a yellow bill, a brown back, a rusty-orange chest, and a whitish ring around the eyes. Females are similar in color but are not as bright as males, and they usually have a brownish head.

Did you know?

The bald eagle is an endangered species success story! The bald eagle was once endangered due to a pesticide called DDT that weakened eggshells and caused them to crack early. Through the banning of DDT and other conservation efforts, the bald eagle population recovered, and it was removed from the Endangered Species List in July of 2007.

Nest Type	Most Active	Migrates

Bald Eagle

Haliaeetus leucocephalus

Size: 3½ feet long; wingspan of 6½–8 feet; weighs 8–14 pounds

Habitat: Forests and tree stands (small forests) near river edges, lakes, seashores, and wetlands

Range: They are a resident bird throughout Wisconsin; they are found throughout much of the US.

Food: Fish, waterfowl (ducks), rabbits, squirrels, muskrats, and deer carcasses; will steal food from other eagles or ospreys

Nesting: Eagles have lifelong partners that begin nesting in fall, laying eggs November–February.

Nest: They build a large nest out of sticks, high up in trees; the nest can be over 5 feet wide and over 6 feet tall, often shaped like an upside-down cone.

Eggs: 1–3 white eggs

Young: Young (chicks) will hatch at around 35 days; young will leave the nest at around 12 weeks. It takes up to 5 years for eagles to get that iconic look!

Predators: Few; collisions with cars sometimes occur.

Migration: They are short-distance migrators, usually to areas with open water; in Wisconsin, many eagles do not migrate at all.

Adult bald eagles have a dark-brown body, a white head and tail, and a golden-yellow beak. Juvenile eagles are mostly brown at first, but their color pattern changes over their first few years. A bald eagle can use its wings as oars to propel itself across bodies of water.

Did you know?

The barred owl has dark-brown eyes; many other owls have yellow eyes. Barred owls, like other owls, have special structures on their primary feathers that allow them to fly silently through the air.

Nest Type

Most Active

Barred Owl

Strix varia

Size: 17–20 inches long; wingspan of 3½ feet; weighs 2 pounds

Habitat: Forested areas, near floodplains of lakes and rivers

Range: They can be found throughout the state of Wisconsin; they are found throughout the eastern US and southern Canada, with scattered populations throughout the Pacific Northwest.

Food: Squirrels, rabbits, and mice; will also prey on birds and aquatic animals like frogs, fish, and crayfish

Nesting: Courtship starts in late fall; nesting starts in winter.

Nest: They use hollow trees; they will also use abandoned nests of other animals and human-made nest structures.

Eggs: 2–4 white eggs with a rough shell

Young: Young (chicks) hatch between 27 and 33 days; they have white down feathers and leave the nest around 5 weeks after hatching. They are fully independent at around 6 months and fully mature at around 2 years.

Predators: Great horned owls, raccoons, weasels, and sometimes northern goshawks feed on eggs and young in the nest.

Migration: Barred owls do not migrate.

The barred owl is a medium-size bird with dark rings highlighting the face. Their feathers are brown and grayish, often with streaking or a bar-like pattern. They have no ear tufts and have a rounded head with a yellow beak and brown eyes. They can easily be identified by their call: "Who cooks for you, who cooks for you all?"

Did you know?
Kingfishers inspired human technology! Bullet trains around the world are designed after the kingfisher's beak, which allows it to dive into water without a splash. This design was used in bullet trains to allow them to enter into tunnels without making a large booming sound. This process of modeling human technology after animal features is called biomimicry.

Nest Type

Most Active

Belted Kingfisher

Megaceryle alcyon

Size: 11–13¾ inches long; wingspan is 19–24 inches; weighs 5–6 ounces

Habitat: Forest and grassland areas near rivers, ponds, lakes

Range: Mostly year-round resident that can be found throughout much of Wisconsin (in the northern part of the state during breeding period) as well as most of the US and Canada

Food: Carnivores, they eat mostly fish and other aquatic animals, such as crayfish and frogs, and occasionally other birds, mammals, and berries.

Nesting: Nests are in the form of upward-sloped burrows that are dug in soft banks on or near water. (The upward slopes prevent flooding.)

Nest: Females and males select the nest site together; males do most of the digging.

Eggs: 5–8 white, smooth, glossy eggs are laid per clutch (group of eggs).

Young: Chicks are born featherless with pink skin, closed eyes, and a dark bill. They receive care from both parents. Chicks leave the nest after about 28 days.

Predators: Snakes, hawks, and mammals

Migration: Mostly a resident bird; in some areas, will migrate south during non-breeding season

The belted kingfisher is bluish gray on top; the bottom half is white with a blue/gray belt or band. The wings have white spots on them. Unlike most other birds, the kingfisher female has a different pattern than the male. Females have a second reddish-brown or rusty-orange band on their belly.

Did you know?

Black-capped chickadees have a unique strategy for surviving winter. The area of the brain that aids in memory (the hippocampus) temporarily gets bigger in preparation for winter. This allows them to remember where they hid or cached seeds.

Nest Type   Most Active

Black-capped Chickadee

Poecile atricapillus

Size: 5½–7½ inches long; wingspan of 8 inches; weighs about half an ounce

Habitat: Forests, woodland edges, and suburban and urban areas

Range: They are year-round residents of Wisconsin and can be found in the northern United States.

Food: Caterpillars, insects, seeds, spiders, and berries

Nesting: March to August

Nest: Chickadees utilize old woodpecker holes or make their own cup-shaped nests in tree cavities that have been weakened by rot.

Eggs: 4–6 eggs that are white with brown spots

Young: Eggs hatch 12–13 days after they are laid; chicks leave the nest around 15 days after hatching, chickadee parents continue feeding the young for another 5–6 weeks.

Predators: Hawks, owls, shrikes, raccoons, house cats left outside, and other mammals

Migration: They do not migrate.

A black-capped chickadee has a gray body with a black cap, or top of head, and a black throat and beak; they have white cheeks and light bellies.

Did you know?

Blue jays get the name "jay" from their noisy and rambunctious personality. Blue jays can mimic; they have been known to copy human speech and often fool birders by mimicking hawks. Sometimes blue jays will mimic hawk calls to scare birds into dropping food. Other possible explanations include using the call to warn other birds that a hawk may be nearby.

Nest Type

Most Active

Blue Jay

Cyanocitta cristata

Size: 11–12½ inches long; wingspan of 16 inches; weighs 2½–3½ ounces

Habitat: Forests and forest edges, suburban areas, city parks, and farm fields

Range: They can be found throughout the state of Wisconsin; their range extends from northeastern and central Canada and well into the West and the Great Plains.

Food: Acorns, seeds, insects, fruits, eggs, nuts, and carrion (dead animals)

Nesting: March to July

Nest: The gathering of nesting materials and the building of nests are shared by both male and female; a cup-shaped nest is built in the fork of tree branches.

Eggs: 4–5 eggs that are either blue or light brown and speckled with brown spots

Young: Chicks hatch naked with eyes closed around 17 days after eggs are laid. Nestlings are cared for by both parents and usually leave the nest 17–20 days after hatching.

Predators: Snakes, crows, falcons, owls, cats, raccoons, and hawks

Migration: Nonmigratory

The blue jay's feathers appear blue, but they are actually brown. They look blue because of refraction, or the bending of light. It has a blue crest (feathers on its head); the underbody is white or gray. A blue jay can hold food items with its feet and use its beak to open them. Sometimes they will store food for later.

Did you know?

Canada geese sometimes travel over 600 miles in a day. They fly in a V formation, which allows them to travel long distances without stopping because they can switch positions. As the lead bird gets tired, it drops to the back of the line and a new bird leads. The V formation helps them communicate and helps prevent collisions.

Nest Type   Most Active   Migrates

Canada Goose

Branta canadensis

Size: 2–3½ feet long; wingspan of 5–6 feet; weighs 6½–20 pounds

Habitat: Ponds, marshes, lakes, parks, and farm fields

Range: They can be found throughout much of Wisconsin as year-round residents and in the north-central areas of the state during the breeding season; they are widespread in the rest of the US.

Food: Omnivores, they eat grasses, aquatic insects, seeds, and some crops, like corn or alfalfa.

Nesting: March to April

Nest: Nests are made on the ground, on elevated areas near the water, or sometimes on a muskrat mound. Nest sites are picked with protection in mind; areas that have clear views and vantage points are more likely to be used.

Eggs: 2–8 cream-colored eggs that are 3 inches long and about 2½ inches wide

Young: Goslings hatch about a month after being laid. They are born with yellow down feathers that they lose as they get older. At the time of hatching, they can swim and walk.

Predators: Mink, raccoons, foxes, dogs, and great horned owls

Migration: A large portion will stay and winter in Wisconsin, while others will fly farther south.

The Canada goose is recognizable by its famous honk and body pattern of brown feathers with a black neck, head, bill, and even feet. They have white cheek feathers. They do fly at night during migration.

Did you know?
Because of the way their legs are situated on their body, loons aren't good at walking on land. Loons have to get a running (or swimming) start to take off from the water.

Nest Type

Most Active

Migrates

Common Loon

Gavia immer

Size: 28–36 inches long; wingspan of 40–55 inches; weighs 3½–13 pounds

Habitat: Quiet freshwater lakes

Range: They can be found throughout northern Wisconsin during breeding season and southern parts of Wisconsin as a migrant; they're found in several other northern states and in Canada during the breeding season, and they're widespread across the US during migration.

Food: Fish, snails, and crayfish

Nesting: May to August

Nest: The male selects the nesting spot; males and females will build a nest out of grasses and reeds together near the water.

Eggs: 2 eggs that have a brown base layer with brown spots

Young: Young (adorably called loonlets) usually hatch in 29 days, covered with dark, fuzzy down; they can swim immediately after hatching. Chicks will ride on a parent's back.

Predators: Mink, raccoons, skunks, other loons, and eagles

Migration: Loons migrate to southern states.

The common loon sports a black-and-white checkered back and a dark green-and-blackish head with red eyes and a black bill. During the fall, adults change a great deal: they lose their checkered spots, the head feathers become gray, and the bill lightens to a dull gray.

Did you know?

Bluebirds are not really blue! The "blue" that we see is visible because of the way that light hits the structure of the feathers, but there is no blue pigment in their feathers. The eastern bluebird will use a large variety of sounds to attract a mate; sometimes, an individual male will sing many different songs per minute!

Nest Type   Most Active   Migrates

Eastern Bluebird

Sialia sialis

Size: 7 inches long; wingspan of 13 inches; weighs 1 ounce

Habitat: Open woodlands, meadows, prairies, gardens, parks, and suburban areas

Range: They can be found in the entire state of Wisconsin during breeding season and throughout the eastern and southern United States.

Food: Berries, insects, and seeds

Nesting: Late March to late July or early August

Nest: Bluebirds utilize woodpecker cavities and other tree holes, as well as nesting boxes. The nest is lined with grasses.

Eggs: Clutch (group of eggs) size is 3–6; eggs are a light blue color.

Young: Chicks hatch mostly featherless and blind. They gain sight in 1 week and have all feathers at around 2 weeks. Chicks will leave the nest at around 3 weeks but will receive care until about 4 weeks.

Predators: House sparrows and European starlings will invade nests and destroy eggs. Eggs and young are preyed upon by house cats, raccoons, rodents, and more.

Migration: They migrate to the southern United States.

Eastern bluebird males are a rich blue with a rusty breast; females are a dull brown with faint blue feathers. Bluebirds are known to return to Wisconsin in March.

Did you know?
The great blue heron is the largest and most common heron species in Wisconsin. A heron's eye color changes as it ages. The eyes start out gray but transition to yellow over time. Great blue herons swallow prey whole.

Nest Type

Most Active

Migrates

Great Blue Heron
Ardea herodias

Size: 3–4½ feet long; wingspan of 6–7 feet; weighs 5–7 pounds

Habitat: Lakes, ponds, rivers, marshes, lagoons, wetlands, and coastal areas like beaches

Range: They can be found throughout Wisconsin, as well as the entire United States and down into Mexico.

Food: Fish, rats, crabs, shrimp, grasshoppers, crayfish, other birds, small mammals, snakes, and lizards

Nesting: May to August

Nest: 2–3 feet across and saucer shaped; often grouped in large rookeries (colonies) in tall trees along the water's edge. Nests are built out of sticks and are often located in dead trees more than 100 feet above the ground; nests are used year after year.

Eggs: 3–7 pale bluish eggs

Young: Chicks will hatch after 28 days of incubation; young will stay in the nest for around 10 weeks. They reach reproductive maturity at just under 2 years.

Predators: Eagles, crows, gulls, raccoons, bears, and hawks

Migration: Populations in northern areas will fly south to southern states, the Caribbean, and Central America.

The great blue heron is a large wading bird with blue and gray upper body feathers; the belly area is white. They have long yellow legs that they use to stalk prey in the water. Great blue herons are famous for stalking prey at the water's edge; their specially adapted feet keep them from sinking into the mud!

Did you know?

A great horned owl can exert a crushing force of over 300 pounds with its talons. Despite its name, the great horned owl doesn't have horns at all. Instead, the obvious tufts on its head are made of feathers. Scientists aren't sure exactly how the tufts function, but they may help them stay hidden.

Nest Type

Most Active

Great Horned Owl

Bubo virginianus

Size: Up to 23 inches long; wingspan of 45 inches; weighs 3 pounds

Habitat: Woods; swamps; desert edges; as well as heavily populated areas such as cities, suburbs, and parks

Range: They are found throughout Wisconsin and the continent of North America.

Food: They eat a variety of foods, but mostly mammals. Sometimes they eat other birds as well.

Nesting: They have lifelong partnerships, with nesting season starting in early winter; egg-laying starts in mid-January to February.

Nest: Nests are found 20–50 feet off the ground. They tend to reuse nests from other raptors or hollowed-out trees.

Eggs: The female lays 2–4 whitish eggs. Eggs are incubated for around 30 days.

Young: Young can fly at around 9 weeks old. The parents care for and feed young for several months.

Predators: Young owls are preyed upon by foxes, coyotes, bears, and opossums. As adults, they are rarely attacked by other birds of prey, such as golden eagles and goshawks.

Migration: Great horned owls are not regular migrators, but some individuals will travel south during the winter.

They are bulky birds with large ear tufts, a rusty brown-to-grayish face with a black border, and large bright eyes. The body color tends to be brown; the wing pattern is checkered with an intermingled dark brown. The chest and belly areas are light brown and have white bars.

Did you know?

Downy woodpeckers are the smallest woodpecker species in North America. Hairy woodpeckers can hear insects traveling under the tree bark. Downy woodpeckers have a built-in mask, or special feathers, near their nostrils that helps them to avoid breathing in wood chips while pecking.

Nest Type   Most Active

Hairy/Downy Woodpecker

Leuconotopicus villosus/Dryobates pubescens

Size: Hairy: 7–10 inches long; wingspan of 13–16 inches; weighs 3 ounces. Downy: 5½–7 inches long; wingspan of 10–12 inches; weighs less than an ounce

Habitat: Forested areas, parks, woodlands, and orchards

Range: Throughout Wisconsin and across the United States

Food: Hairy: beetles, ants, caterpillars, fruits, and seeds. Downy: beetles, ants, galls, wasps, seeds, and berries

Nesting: Hairy: April to July. Downy: April to July

Nest: In both woodpecker species, pairs will work together to create a cavity. Both parents also help to incubate eggs.

Eggs: Hairy: 3–7 white eggs. Downy: 3–8 white eggs

Young: Hairy woodpeckers' eggs will hatch 2 weeks after being laid and then fledge (develop enough feathers to fly) after another month. Downy woodpeckers' eggs will hatch after about 12 days and fledge 18–21 days after hatching. Both species hatch blind and featherless.

Predators: American kestrels, snakes, sharp-shinned hawks, pet cats, rats, squirrels, and Cooper's hawks

Migration: Woodpeckers are mostly year-round residents, but some in the north may travel south during the winter.

Hairy woodpeckers and downy woodpeckers look strikingly similar with their color pattern. One way to distinguish them is to look at the size of the body and bill. The downy woodpecker is smaller than the hairy woodpecker and has a shorter bill. If you look at the tail feathers of the two species, you will also see that the hairy woodpecker does not have black spots, while the downy's tail does.

Did you know?

Groups of hooded merganser ducklings will avoid being attacked by raptors by mimicking the shape of a swimming muskrat. The merganser is one of the few duck species in our area that eats lots of fish; it can dive underwater for up to two minutes while fishing.

Nest Type

Most Active

Migrates

Hooded Merganser

Lophodytes cucullatus

Size: Up to 1½ feet long; wingspan of 2 feet; weighs 1–2 pounds

Habitat: Wooded lakes and streams, marshes, small rivers, and woodlands adjacent to bodies of water

Range: They can be found throughout the northern parts of Wisconsin during the breeding season; in southern parts they are year-round residents. Several populations can be found across the United States and Canada.

Food: Fish, tadpoles, aquatic insects, and crustaceans

Nesting: April to June

Nest: Nests are shallow, bowl shaped, and made inside tree cavities or human-made wooden duck-nesting structures. Down feathers and wood chips are added to the cavity.

Eggs: 10–12 white eggs

Young: After a month of incubation, eggs will hatch, and ducklings will leave the nest within 24 hours of hatching. They can fly after about 65 days.

Predators: Hawks, humans, snakes, mink, and martens

Migration: Some populations migrate south for the winter, while others will migrate north and overwinter on the Great Lakes.

Hooded merganser males have a black-and-white crest that can help distinguish them from females. Other identifying features include brilliant yellow eyes, black-and-white feathers on its breast and back, and a brown side. The females are duller with a brown crest on the back of the head, brown feathers, and brown eyes.

Did you know?

When viewed straight-on, the yellow portion on the mallard's bill resembles a cartoon dog's head. Most domesticated ducks share the mallard as their ancestor. Mallard feathers are waterproof; they use oil from the preen gland beneath their feathers to help aid in repelling water. Mallards are the most common duck in the United States.

Nest Type

Most Active

Migrates

Mallard
Anas platyrhynchos

Size: 24 inches long; wingspan of 36 inches; weighs 2½–3 pounds

Habitat: Lakes, ponds, rivers, and marshes

Range: They are found throughout Wisconsin; the population stretches across the United States and Canada into Mexico and as far up as central Alaska.

Food: Insects, worms, snails, aquatic vegetation, sedge seeds, grasses, and wild rice

Nesting: April to August

Nest: The nest is constructed on the ground, usually near a body of water.

Eggs: 9–13 eggs

Young: Eggs hatch 26–28 days after being laid. The ducklings are fully feathered and have the ability to swim at the time of hatching. Ducklings are cared for until they're 2–3 months old and reach reproductive maturity at 1 year old.

Predators: Humans, crows, mink, coyotes, raccoons, and snapping turtles

Migration: After breeding season, a lot of the population will migrate south; others will stay in familiar areas that have adequate food and shelter.

Male mallards are gray with an iridescent green head with a tinge of purple spotting, a white line along the collar, rusty-brown chest, yellow bill, and orange legs and feet. Females are dull brown with a yellow bill, a bluish area near the tail, and orange feet.

Did you know?

A mourning dove eats around 12% or more of its body weight each day. Mourning doves will store seeds and grain in their crop (pouch on their neck). Some people mistake the mourning dove call for an owl call.

Nest Type Most Active

Mourning Dove
Zenaida macroura

Size: 8–14 inches long; wingspan of 17–19 inches; weighs 3½–6 ounces

Habitat: Woodlands, parks, grasslands, scrub areas, farm fields, and suburban and urban areas

Range: In Wisconsin, it can be found throughout the state; it is abundant throughout southern Canada and the continental United States.

Food: Fruits, insects, and seeds; young feed on crop milk

Nesting: Courtship begins in April.

Nest: Males will show females several potential nesting sites. The female will choose the site, the male will bring nest-building materials to the female, and she will then construct the nest.

Eggs: 2 white eggs, incubated by both parents

Young: Within 2 weeks, hatchlings will depart the nest, but they receive care for another week or so.

Predators: Cats, falcons, hawks, raccoons, and humans

Migration: Year-round in much of Wisconsin, except the far north, where breeding populations are found in the summer.

Mourning doves are gray and brown. They have a brown chest and pointed tail that has a white tip on it. Their beak is grayish-black, the eyes are black, and on their head just below the eyes they have a black spot. They can be recognized by their spooky "hoo, hoo, hoo" call or the whistling of their wings when they take off.

Did you know?

Cardinals are very territorial and will sometimes attack their own reflection thinking that it is another cardinal that has entered its territory. The early bird gets the worm, and cardinals are some of the first birds active in the morning.

Nest Type   Most Active

Northern Cardinal

Cardinalis cardinalis

Size: 8–9 inches long; wingspan of 12 inches

Habitat: Hardwood forests, urban areas, orchards, backyards, and fields

Range: They are found throughout Wisconsin, as well as the eastern and midwestern parts of the United States.

Food: Seeds, fruits, insects, spiders, and centipedes

Nesting: March to August

Nest: The cup-shaped nest is built by females in thick foliage, usually at least 1 foot off the ground. It can be 3 inches tall and 4 inches wide.

Eggs: The female lays 2–5 off-white eggs with a variety of colored speckles.

Young: About 2 weeks after eggs are laid, chicks hatch with their eyes closed and mostly naked, aside from sparsely placed down feathers.

Predators: Hawks, owls, and squirrels

Migration: Cardinals do not migrate.

Northern cardinal males are bright-red birds with a black face. Females are a washed-out red or brown in color. Both males and females have a crest (tuft of feathers on the head), an orange beak, and grayish legs. Cardinals can be identified by their laser-gun-like call.

Did you know?

Northern shovelers get their name from their shovel-shaped bill. When northern shovelers take flight, a rattling sound is produced by their wings.

Nest Type

Most Active

Migrates

Northern Shoveler

Spatula clypeata

Size: 19–20 inches long; wingspan of 30–33 inches; weighs 15–29 ounces

Habitat: Lakes, estuaries, coastal shorelines, salt marshes, flooded fields, and agricultural ponds

Range: Throughout Wisconsin and the Northeast during migration; throughout North America at various times of the year.

Food: Aquatic insects, crustaceans, and small fish; seeds and aquatic plants during winter

Nesting: April to June

Nest: Females build a depression nest on the ground that is about 8 inches wide, lined with down feathers and filled with dried grasses and weeds.

Eggs: A brood or clutch of 9–12 pale-olive eggs about 2 inches long and 1½ inches wide is laid.

Young: Chicks hatch about 25 days after laying. They are precocial, meaning they are fully developed and able to swim and walk shortly after hatching. After 40 days or so, they will begin to fly and become independent.

Predators: Red foxes, raccoons, owls, hawks, large gulls, mink, weasels, skunks, coyotes, and crows

Migration: Most often seen during migration, but some nest in east-central Wisconsin.

Males in their breeding plumage sport an iridescent green head, brown belly and sides, and white chest. They have blue forewings that are visible when in flight. Females and nonbreeding males are brown with a gray-hued bill. The juvenile's bill will turn into the classic shoveler shape as it matures.

Did you know?

The osprey is nicknamed the "fish hawk" because it is the only hawk in North America that mainly eats live fish. An osprey will rotate its catch to put it in line with its body, pointing headfirst, which allows for less resistance in flight as the air travels over the fish.

Nest Type

Most Active

Migrates

Osprey
Pandion haliaetus

Size: 21–23 inches long; wingspan of 59–71 inches; weighs 3–4½ pounds

Habitat: Near lakes, ponds, rivers, swamps, and reservoirs

Range: Wisconsin during the breeding and migration season; throughout the US and Canada and Alaska

Food: Feeds mostly on fish; they sometimes eat mammals, birds, and reptiles if there are few fish.

Nesting: For ospreys that migrate, egg-laying happens in April and May. The female will take on most of the incubation of the eggs, as well as the jobs of keeping the offspring warm and providing protection.

Nest: Platform nests are constructed out of twigs and sticks. Nests are constructed on trees, snags, or human-made objects like cellular towers and telephone poles.

Eggs: The mother lays 1–3 cream-colored eggs; they have splotches of various shades of brown and pinkish red on them.

Young: Chicks hatch after around 36 days and have brown-and-white down feathers. Ospreys fledge around 50–55 days after hatching and will receive care from parents for another 2 months or so.

Predators: Owls, eagles, foxes, skunks, raccoons, and snakes

Migration: Ospreys migrate south to wintering areas in the fall.

Ospreys are raptors, and they have a brown upper body and white lower body. The wings are brown on the outside and white on the underside, with brown spotting and streaks toward the edge. The head is white with a brown band that goes through the eye area, highlighting the yellow eyes.

Did you know?

The red-tailed hawk is the most abundant hawk in North America. The red-tailed hawk's scream is the sound effect that you hear when soaring eagles are shown in movies. Eagles do not screech like hawks, so filmmakers use hawk calls instead! Red-tailed hawks can't move their eyes, so they have to move their entire head in order to get a better view around them.

Nest Type   Most Active   Migrates

Red-tailed Hawk (RT)/ Red-shouldered Hawk (RS)

Buteo jamaicensis / Buteo lineatus

Size: RT: 19–25 inches long; wingspan of 47–57 inches; weighs 2½–4 pounds. RS: 16½–24 inches long; wingspan of 37–43 inches; weighs around 1 pound

Habitat: RT: Deserts, woodlands, fields. RS: Forests, swamps, grasslands, urban areas

Range: Year-round residents throughout much of Wisconsin. RT: throughout North America during breeding season. RS: throughout eastern US during breeding season.

Food: RT: Rodents, birds, reptiles, bats, and insects. RS: Small mammals, lizards, snakes, crayfish, songbirds

Nesting: Hawks mate for life; nesting starts in March.

Nest: RT: Both parents build a large cup shaped nest, made of sticks and branches. RS: Both parents build a cup-shaped nest 20 feet off the ground.

Eggs: RT: White with colored blotches. RS: Off-white or slightly blue with varied markings

Young: RT: Young hatch after 30 days. They can fly at 5–6 weeks. RS: Chicks can fly after 5–6 weeks.

Predators: RT: Owls and crows. RS: Snakes, mammals, and owls

Migration: Birds in the northern areas of range will migrate short distances to warmer areas, while the hawks in the southern part of the state do not migrate.

Red-tailed hawks are named for their rusty-red tails! They have brown heads and a light-brown chest with brown streaking. Red-shouldered hawks have a reddish-brown head and back, with rusty undersides with white barring across the belly.

Did you know?
Red-winged blackbirds are one of the most abundant songbirds in the United States. Sometimes their winter roost (colony) can have several thousand to up to a million birds. In many areas, red-winged blackbirds are considered a pest because of their love of grain and seeds from farm fields. In others, they are welcomed because they eat insects that are considered pests to farmers.

Nest Type

Most Active

Migrates

98

Red-winged Blackbird

Agelaius phoeniceus

Size: 7–9½ inches long; wingspan of 13 inches; weighs 2 ounces

Habitat: Marshes, lakeshores, meadows, parks, and open fields

Range: Throughout Wisconsin; some are breeding residents in northern Wisconsin, while some, especially in southern Wisconsin, are year-round residents; ranges from central Canada through the US and into Mexico.

Food: Dragonflies, spiders, beetles, snails, seeds, and fruits

Nesting: February to August

Nest: Female builds a cup from plant material.

Eggs: 3–4 eggs that come in a variety of colors, from pale blue to gray with black-and-brown spots or streaks

Young: Chicks hatch blind and naked after around 12 days of incubation. Hatchlings will leave the nest after 12 days but will continue to receive care for another 5 weeks.

Predators: Raccoons, mink, owls, and raptors

Migration: Far north populations migrate south during the winter, but some do not migrate.

Red-winged blackbird males are a sleek black with an orangish-red spot that overlays a dandelion-yellow spot on the wings. Females have a combination of dark-brown and light-brown streaks throughout the body. Male red-winged blackbirds spend much of breeding season defending their territory from other males and attacking predators or anything else that gets too close to the nest.

Did you know?

A group of gulls is called a squabble. Ring-billed gulls use the Earth's magnetic field to navigate, and they often return very close (a matter of feet) to their nesting area. They can reach speeds over 35 miles per hour (mph) and can snatch food out of the air, even the occasional meal of a beachgoer!

Nest Type

Most Active

Migrates

Ring-billed Gull

Larus delawarensis

Size: 17–21 inches long; wingspan of 41–46 inches; weighs 10½–24½ ounces

Habitat: Beaches, mudflats, urban and suburban areas

Range: Can be found during the breeding season throughout much of the state and in the southernmost western part of the state during migration. Found in Canada and the Pacific Northwest in summer

Food: Fish, crabs, rodents, insects, grains, and fruits

Nesting: Ground nesters; breeds in colonies

Nest: Both sexes build a shallow cup nest of vegetation on the ground by bodies of water. Nests are built on sand, sandbars, and rock-filled beaches.

Eggs: 2–4 light greenish-gray eggs with brown specks; eggs are about 2–2½ inches long and 1½ inches wide.

Young: Chicks hatch after 20–30 days; both parents take care of chicks. Chicks can fly around 5 weeks after hatching and are fully independent at that point.

Predators: Coyotes, raccoons, striped skunks, mink, and red foxes; other birds

Migration: Migrates in flocks from Canada, Wisconsin, and other northern states before wintering in the southern US and Mexico.

The male and female ringed-billed gulls look the same. They have a yellow bill with a black ring just shy of the tip; their head is white, the body gray with gray wings and black-tipped flight feathers. Adults have yellow feet and eyes as well.

Did you know?

Rose-breasted grosbeaks are famous for their melodic songs. During the mating season, males may sing up to 689 songs in a day while advertising their breeding territories. Rose-breasted grosbeaks are very strong fliers; during migration, they are able to fly across the Gulf of Mexico without stopping, which is over 500 miles (805 km)!

Nest Type

Most Active

Migrates

Rose-breasted Grosbeak

Pheucticus ludovicianus

Size: 7–8½ inches long; wingspan of 11½–13 inches; weighs 1½–2 ounces

Habitat: Forests, forest edges, shrubby areas, swamps, and other wetlands

Range: Can be found throughout Wisconsin and much of the northeastern United States. During the breeding season, it is a common bird in portions of the Midwest; during migration, it's common in the eastern US.

Food: Omnivores that eat mostly insects and other invertebrates (animals without bones) like spiders and snails. Seeds are also a big portion of their diet.

Nesting: Females lay 1 or 3 broods (groups) of 3–5 eggs a year. Both parents incubate and provide care to young.

Nest: Cup-shaped nest built out of twigs, weeds, and leaves

Eggs: Light greenish or bluish eggs that can be spotted with a brownish red

Young: Chicks are born with just a small number of feathers about 11 days after laying. They will leave the nest 9–12 days after hatching and will be completely independent around the 3-week mark.

Predators: Blue jays, hawks, grackles, and squirrels

Migration: Migrates twice a year in the spring and fall, usually flying during the night hours

Males and females have different appearances, with the male having a white bill, black head, and a white belly with a rose-colored throat that extends down towards parts of the white breast. Females are not as colorful; they have a brown back and off-white-to-cream-colored belly with brown streaks.

Did you know?

Snow geese are extreme travelers; some will travel over 2,200 miles during migration. As hatchlings, they may walk over 50 miles from their nest to areas better suited for growing.

Nest Type

Most Active

Migrates

Snow Goose

Anser caerulescens

Size: 27–32½ inches long; wingspan of 54½ inches; weighs 56½–116 ounces

Habitat: Marshes, prairies, fields, islands, estuaries, tidal flats, farmland, ponds, and shallow lakes

Range: Can be found throughout Wisconsin during migration; they can also be found throughout the Midwest and Canada during migration and breed in arctic Canada and Alaska.

Food: Herbivore that feeds on plants and seeds. During migration, will eat grains and stems from farmlands. Young sometimes eat fruit and insect larvae.

Nesting: May to June

Nest: Females build a scrape nest on the ground lined with down feathers and vegetation.

Eggs: Usually 2–6 oval or elongated white eggs, about 3 inches long and 2 inches wide.

Young: Chicks hatch with eyes opened with downy feathers about 25 days after laying.

Predators: Eagles, foxes, wolves, common ravens, gulls, dogs, bears, and humans

Migration: They migrate south from far northern Canada and Alaska, spending winters in southern Canada, and the northern US.

Snow geese have white bodies with black wing tips. They have a pink- to ruby-orange bill with a dark streak, giving the appearance of lips. Sometimes snow geese will have a different plumage of a dark or brown body with a white head and white undertail. This plumage is known as a dark morph.

Did you know?

Snowy owls are one of the few species of owls that are diurnal, which means they hunt during the daytime, while most of the other owls hunt at night. Snowy owls can hunt over 1,500 lemmings (small rodents related to voles) in a single year. Because of their thick feathers, snowy owls are the largest owls in North America by weight.

Nest Type

Most Active

Migrates

Snowy Owl

Bubo scandiacus

Size: 20½–28 inches; wingspan of 49½–57 inches; weighs 56½–104 ounces

Habitat: Prairies, fields, marshes, farmland

Range: During the winter, they can be found throughout the state of Wisconsin; they can also be found throughout New England and westward to Washington state.

Food: Small mammals, especially lemmings (a rodent). They also eat birds.

Nesting: Snowy owls usually breed during the months of May and September. Males court females using a mix of displays, one performed while in the air and the other performed while on the ground.

Nest: Female builds the nest by hollowing out an area on the ground and using her body to make the nest shape.

Eggs: Usually 3–11 white eggs, about 2 inches long and wide, are laid per brood.

Young: Chicks or owlets hatch blind with downy feathers 30 days after laying. Chicks receive care from both parents. After about 14–25 days, chicks will venture out from the nest.

Predators: Foxes, wolves, dogs, and humans

Migration: They migrate south from far northern Canada and Alaska, spending winters in southern Canada, and the northern US.

Snowy owls are white with brown bars and spots. The males are a more brilliant and vibrant white, while the females are darker in color with more spots and bars than the males. Both males and females have bright-yellow eyes.

Did you know?

The trumpeter swan is the largest and heaviest waterfowl species found in North America. Trumpeter swans will use their webbed feet to aid in egg incubation. When feeding on deep aquatic plants, they will create a current in the water by pumping their feet; this current allows them to pull aquatic plants from the bottom more easily.

Nest Type   Most Active   Migrates

Trumpeter Swan
Cygnus buccinator

Size: 60–72 inches long; wingspan of 72–84 inches; weighs 17–28 pounds

Habitat: Lakes, rivers, marshes, wetlands, and coastal areas

Range: They are found in various parts of Wisconsin, with certain portions of the state having higher densities than others. They can also be found in isolated populations throughout the northern United States and Canada.

Food: Aquatic plants, small fish, crustaceans, and fish eggs

Nesting: April to June

Nest: Both male and female swans construct the circular nest. Nest-building can take 2–5 weeks to complete.

Eggs: 4–6 cream or white eggs

Young: Young hatch 32–37 days after eggs are laid; they leave the nest after a day and can fly after around 100 days. They are independent at around 10 months and reach full maturity between 4 and 7 years.

Predators: Eagles, owls, coyotes, mink, otters, and ravens

Migration: Northern populations will move south in winter to areas with open water.

Adult trumpeter swans are large white birds with long necks, black bills, and webbed feet; juveniles (young) are a grayish color. Trumpeter swans are only found in North America. They have a thick layer of down feathers that aid in living in cold areas.

Did you know?

The whooping crane is named for the whooping sound it makes, which it uses to communicate and alert others of danger. It is an endangered species; at one time, the population was as low as 15 birds, but now through the help of conservation efforts like reintroductions, there are over 500 birds in the wild. Some populations learn to migrate by following a small aircraft during their first migration.

Nest Type   Most Active   Migrates

Whooping Crane

Grus americana

Size: 59 inches long; wingspan of 90 inches; weighs 13¼–17 pounds

Habitat: Lakes, rivers, marshes, grasslands, croplands, wetlands, and coastal areas

Range: They can be found in the eastern United States; in Wisconsin, they can be found in the central part of the state. They were reintroduced.

Food: Omnivorous; plants, berries, insects, seeds, small fish, crustaceans, frogs, and small mammals

Nesting: March–May; they form lifelong breeding pairs around year 2 or 3.

Nest: Both male and female construct a mound nest usually with a flat top or shallow depression hidden by brush and other vegetation.

Eggs: 1–3 olive or light-brown eggs with brown patches

Young: Chicks hatch 29–31 days after eggs are laid. They can swim and walk several hours after hatching. They will leave the nest after around 80–90 days.

Predators: Eagles, coyotes, raccoons (eat the eggs), bears, and humans

Migration: Migrate during the breeding season

Whooping cranes are large birds with long legs and a long neck. They have a thick, straight, tan bill that usually has a black tip. Adults are brilliant white; their head is black with highlights of red over it, especially around the bill and top of head. Juveniles are white with splotches of cinnamon brown; their wings are white, while adults have black wing tips. The overall slender body widens to a plump "bustle" at the tail.

Did you know?

Turkeys sometimes fly at night, unlike most birds, and land in trees to roost. Turkeys have some interesting facial features; the red skin growth on a turkey's face above the beak is called a snood, while the growth under the beak is called a wattle. Wild turkeys can have more than 5,000 feathers.

Nest Type   Most Active

Wild Turkey

Meleagris gallopavo

Size: 3–4 feet long; wingspan of 5 feet; males weigh 16–25 pounds; females weigh 9–11 pounds.

Habitat: Woodlands and grasslands

Range: Found throughout Wisconsin. They also can be found in the eastern US and have been introduced in many western areas of the country.

Food: Grain, snakes, frogs, insects, acorns, berries, and ferns

Nesting: April to September

Nest: The nest is built on the ground using leaves as bedding, in brush or near the base of trees or fallen logs.

Eggs: 10–12 tan eggs with very small reddish-brown spots

Young: Poults (young) hatch about a month after eggs are laid; they will flock with the mother for a year. When young are still unable to fly, the mom will stay on the ground with her poults to provide protection and warmth. When poults grow up, they are known as hens if they are female, or as gobblers or toms if they are male.

Predators: Humans, foxes, raccoons, owls, eagles, skunks, and fishers

Migration: Turkeys do not migrate.

A wild turkey is a large bird that is dark brown and black with some iridescent feathers. Males will fan out their tail to attract a mate. When threatened, they will also fan out their tail and rush the predator, sometimes kicking and puncturing prey with the spurs on their feet.

Did you know?

Wood ducks will "mimic" a soccer player when a predator is near their young: they flop! Female wood ducks will fake a broken wing to lure predators away from her young. Wood duck hatchlings must jump from the nest after hatching to reach the water. They can jump 50 feet or more without hurting themselves.

Nest Type

Most Active

Migrates

Wood Duck

Aix sponsa

Size: 15–20 inches long; wingspan of 30 inches; weighs about a pound

Habitat: Swamps, woody ponds, and marshes

Range: They are year-long residents throughout much of Wisconsin. In northern Wisconsin, they are breeding residents. They are also in the eastern US, southern Mexico, the Pacific Northwest, and on the West Coast.

Food: Fruits; nuts; and aquatic vegetation, especially duckweed, sedges, and grasses

Nesting: March to August

Nest: Wood ducks use hollow trees, abandoned woodpecker cavities, and human-made nesting boxes.

Eggs: 8–15 off-white eggs are laid once a year. Sometimes females will lay eggs in another female's nest; this process is called egg dumping.

Young: Eggs hatch about a month after being laid. Chicks will leave the nest after a day and fly within 8 weeks.

Predators: Raccoons, mink, fish, hawks, snapping turtles, owls, humans, and muskrats

Migration: Mostly a year-round resident, populations in northern areas migrate during the breeding season.

Wood duck males have a brightly colored crest (tuft of feathers) of iridescent (shimmering) green, red, and purple, with a mahogany (brown) upper breast area and tan bottom. Males also have red eyes. Females are brown to gray. Wood ducks have strong claws that enable them to climb up trees into cavities.

Did you know?
The American toad is the most commonly observed toad in Wisconsin. While the American toad has warts on it, you cannot get warts from touching it. Toads are toxic (but not to humans); they have two parotid glands—one behind each eye that produces a toxin they release to prevent predators from eating them.

Most Active

Hibernates

American Toad

Anaxyrus americanus

Size: 2–4 inches long; weighs 1½–2 ounces

Habitat: Prairies, forests, suburban areas, swamps, and other wetlands

Range: They are found throughout Wisconsin and from New England south into parts of Mississippi, Alabama, and Georgia.

Food: Insects, worms, snails, ants, moths, and beetles

Mating: February to July

Nest: No nest

Eggs: 2,000–19,000 or more eggs are laid in bodies of water attached to vegetation or the bottom of shallow water.

Young: Eggs hatch 3–10 days after laying. They will stay in the tadpole stage 40–65 days. It takes 2–3 years to reach reproductive maturity.

Predators: Hognoses and other snakes, raccoons, and birds; as tadpoles: beetles, crayfish, birds, and dragonfly larvae

The American toad has a brown-to-clay-red colored base layer with brown and black spots and noticeable warts on its body. During the summer or extreme heat, toads can reduce their metabolic rate and cool themselves down.

Did you know?

Eastern garter snakes are highly social and will form groups with other snakes and often other species to overwinter together in a burrow or hole. When threatened by a predator or handled, they will sometimes musk or emit a foul-smelling, oily substance from their cloaca (butt).

Most Active   Hibernates

Eastern Garter Snake

Thamnophis sirtalis

Size: 14–36 inches long (rarely over 17 inches); weighs 5–5½ ounces

Habitat: Forests and forest edges, grasslands, and suburban areas

Range: They are found throughout Wisconsin and can be found in the eastern US from Minnesota, southward to eastern Texas, and then east towards the Atlantic coast.

Food: Frogs, snails, toads, salamanders, insects, fish, and worms

Mating: April or May

Nest: No nest; they will use natural cavities in the ground or abandoned burrows of small mammals.

Eggs: No eggs are laid. Eastern garter snakes are born live in a litter of 8–20 snakes.

Young: Snakelets are 4½–9 inches long at birth; no parental care is given.

Predators: Crows, ravens, hawks, owls, raccoons, foxes, and squirrels

Eastern garter snakes are black with three yellow stripes running down their body on the back and sides. They withstand winter by gathering in groups inside the burrows of rodents or under human-made structures, and they enter brumation, or a state of slowed body activity.

119

Did you know?

The eastern hognose snake is venomous! But its venom is not harmful to us. The hognose's teeth have a dual purpose: they inject venom into prey and also deflate toads who puff their bodies up to avoid being eaten. The hognose wards off would-be predators by flattening its head to look like a cobra. If that doesn't work, it will play dead by flipping its body over and letting its tongue hang out of its mouth.

Most Active   Hibernates

Eastern Hognose Snake

Heterodon platirhinos

Size: 2–2½ feet long; weighs 2–4 ounces

Habitat: Shrublands, prairies, grasslands, coastal areas, and forests

Range: The hognose can be found throughout Wisconsin, except the pockets in the northern and eastern part of the state. It has an expansive range southward into Florida and westward into Texas and parts of Kansas.

Food: Frogs, toads, salamanders, birds, and invertebrates

Mating: April and May

Nest: Eastern hognose snakes dig burrows and will lay eggs under rocks, leaves, or in rotting logs.

Eggs: In June to July they will dig a burrow and lay 8–40 eggs (average clutch is around 25).

Young: 60 days after being laid, the eggs hatch. They do not receive care from parents at birth. Snakes reach full maturity around 20 months.

Predators: Hawks, snakes, raccoons, and opossums

The eastern hognose is a thick-bodied snake that gets its name from its shovel-like snout that it uses to dig in soil. They come in a variety of colors from red and brown to gray and black; they even come in versions of orange and red. Their underbody is lighter than their top.

Did you know?

The eastern massasauga rattlesnake is one of only two venomous snakes that calls Wisconsin home. It is also known as the "swamp rattler" because it is often found in or close to swamp areas. Eastern massasaugas rarely strike humans; instead, they prefer to stay still and hide, sometimes not even rattling because they could be discovered. **Safety Note:** These snakes are venomous (toxic). If you see one, observe or admire it from a distance.

Most Active   Hibernates

Eastern Massasauga Rattlesnake

Sistrurus catenatus

Size: 23–30 inches long; weighs 10½–14 ounces

Habitat: Swamps, marshes, bogs, wetlands, as well as meadows, wet prairies, and grasslands

Range: Massasaugas can be found throughout the states that touch the Great Lakes, as well as portions of Canada, Iowa, and Missouri. In Wisconsin, they can be found in the central and southern parts of the state.

Food: Small snakes, small mammals such as rodents, lizards, and invertebrates like centipedes

Mating: The massasauga's breeding season happens in the spring but can also occur in the fall.

Nest: Abandoned mammal dens or downed logs

Eggs: Does not produce eggs; gives live birth to young

Young: 3–3½ months after mating, 5–20 snakelets are born via live birth in abandoned burrows or downed logs. Young are fully developed when born and will only stay a few days with mom before venturing out on their own. They become mature around 3 or 4 years old.

Predators: Humans, raptors, wild cats

Eastern massasaugas come in a variety of colors from gray and light brown to deep brown and black with dark-colored patches with a light outline around them. They have thick bodies with an arrow- or triangle-shaped head. They have cat-like eyes or vertical pupils. At the base of the tail is a rattle the snake uses to alert would-be threats of its presence.

Did you know?

The eastern newt starts its life in the water and then lives on land as a juvenile before returning to live out the rest of its life in the water as an adult. Some newts will skip the juvenile stage and change straight into an adult. Eastern newts have a toxin that they release through their skin that makes potential predators sick. The bright-orange color of an eastern newt acts as a warning system to would-be predators that they taste bad or are toxic.

Most Active   Hibernates

Eastern Newt

Notophthalmus viridescens

Size: 3–5 inches long; weighs less than a dime

Habitat: Near and in streams, marshes, lakes, and ponds; in woodlands or woody areas

Range: Throughout much of Wisconsin; found from New England and the Atlantic Coast and west as far as Texas

Food: Aquatic insects, snails, worms, amphibians, and fish eggs

Mating: Breeding season for the eastern newt starts in the winter and finishes in early spring.

Nest: No true nest; eggs are laid underwater.

Eggs: Females lay eggs in the spring, in still or quiet water. Eggs attach to underwater vegetation. Females lay 200–400 eggs, providing no form of care.

Young: The larvae hatch around 3–8 weeks after eggs are laid. Larvae transform into efts (juveniles) by the end of summer. Efts live on land for 1–3 years. When mature, they return to the water for the remainder of their lives.

Predators: Fish, birds, insects, amphibians, and reptiles

The eastern newt goes through three life stages. It has a fully aquatic or water-living stage as a larva. During this stage, it has gills and a flat tail. In the next stage (the juvenile stage), it lives on land. This stage of life is called the red eft stage. During this stage, it sports rough, bright-red skin with red spots and has a rounded tail. The last stage is the adult stage, where it has a brownish-yellow-to-olive-brown color on the upper half of the body, red spots outlined by black circles, and a yellow underside with black spots on it.

Did you know?

The eastern tiger salamander can grow up to 13 inches long and live over 20 years! Eastern tiger salamanders migrate to their birthplace in order to breed, sometimes over a mile or more. Eastern tiger salamanders have a hidden weapon! They produce a poisonous toxin that is secreted or released from two glands in their tail. This toxin makes them taste bad to predators and allows them to escape.

Most Active   Hibernates

Eastern Tiger Salamander

Ambystoma tigrinum

Size: 7–13 inches long; weighs 4½ ounces

Habitat: Woodlands, marshes, and meadows; they spend most of their time underground in burrows.

Range: Mostly found in the eastern US. In Wisconsin, they can be found along the band that stretches from the southeastern to the west-central corner. Small populations are also found in the western US.

Food: Carnivores (eaters of meat); insects, frogs, worms, and snails

Mating: Tiger salamanders leave their burrows to find standing bodies of fresh water. They breed in late winter and early spring after the ground has thawed.

Nest: No nest, but eggs are joined together into one group in a jelly-like sack called an egg mass. An egg mass is attached to grass, leaves, and other plant material at the bottom of a pond.

Eggs: There are 20–100 eggs or more in an egg mass.

Young: Eggs hatch after 2 weeks, and the young are fully aquatic with external gills. Limbs develop shortly after hatching; within 3 months, the young are fully grown but will hang around in a vernal pool. Individuals living in permanent ponds can take up to 6 months to fully develop.

Predators: Adults: snakes, owls, and badgers; young: diving beetles, fish, turtles, and herons

Eastern tiger salamanders have thick black, brown, or grayish bodies with uneven spots of yellow, tan, brown, or green along the head and body. The underside is usually a variation of yellow. Males are usually larger and thicker than females.

Did you know?
The gray tree frog looks similar to the Cope's gray tree frog, and you can only tell them apart by listening to their call or looking at their DNA in a lab. Tree frogs are excellent climbers; they have toe pads that help them to climb trees and other structures.

Most Active   Hibernates

Gray Tree Frog

Dryophytes versicolor

Size: 1½–2¼ inches long; weighs ¼ ounce

Habitat: Urban areas, woodlands, and forests

Range: In Wisconsin, they can be found throughout the state. They are also found throughout the eastern United States from the Atlantic Coast to middle Texas, and as far north as southern Canada.

Food: Tadpoles: algae and decaying material in bodies of water; adults: insects, spiders, snails, and slugs

Mating: May to July, in shallow wetlands near forest. Males will call to attract females. Males are territorial and will defend territories with force by headbutting, pushing, and/or kicking other males until they leave.

Nest: No nest is constructed; they will lay several clusters containing around 30 eggs or more on vegetation near the surface of a body of water.

Eggs: Lays 1,000–2,000 eggs

Young: Eggs hatch around 3 weeks after being laid; it takes around 4–8 weeks after hatching to go through metamorphosis. Young reach maturity at around 2 years.

Predators: Skunks, snakes, raccoons, fish, and other frogs

Gray tree frogs can be a variation of colors from gray to shades of green and brown. They are nocturnal, so they are active at night. In winter, they will hibernate in trees. They will produce glycerol, which is a compound that replaces the water in cells to act as an antifreeze during the winter.

Did you know?
Leopard frogs are used by humans in many ways, including in research for medical projects, as well as serving as specimens for biology courses. During the winter, they will hibernate underwater in ponds that have lots of oxygen and do not freeze.

Most Active   Hibernates

Northern Leopard Frog

Lithobates pipiens

Size: 2½–4½ inches long; weighs ½–3 ounces

Habitat: Meadows, open fields, lakes, forest edges, and ponds

Range: They are found throughout Wisconsin; there are strong populations into Canada and throughout the northeastern states to Iowa, with populations extending into northern California, the Pacific Northwest, and the Southwest.

Food: Spiders, worms, insects, and other invertebrates like crustaceans and mollusks

Mating: Late March to early June; mating occurs in water.

Nest: No nest is constructed; within 3 days of mating, the female will lay eggs in permanent shallow bodies of water, attached to vegetation just below the surface.

Eggs: A few hundred to 5,000 or more eggs are laid in one egg mass that is 2–5 inches wide.

Young: Tadpoles hatch about 2–3 weeks after eggs are laid and then complete the metamorphic cycle to become frogs in around 3 months. They reach reproductive maturity in the first or second year for males and within 2–3 years for females.

Predators: Fish, frogs, herons, snakes, hawks, gulls, mink, turtles, and dragonfly larvae

The northern leopard frog is a smooth-skinned frog with 2–3 rows of dark spots with a lighter outline around them, atop a brown or green base layer. It has a ridge that extends from the base of the eye to the rear of the frog. They have a white underside. Juveniles (young) will use streams and drainage ditches with vegetation to reach seasonal habitats.

Did you know?

While ornate box turtles are mainly land dwellers, they are able to float and swim decently due to fat deposits under their shells. During the winter, they bury themselves in sandy soil to avoid freezing.

Most Active   Hibernates

Ornate Box Turtle

Terrapene ornata

Size: 4½–5 inches long; weighs ½–1½ pounds

Habitat: Forests, open grasslands, pastures, shrublands, wetlands, farm fields, and marsh meadows

Range: Can be found as far north as Wisconsin, as far east as Louisiana, as far west as Arizona, and as far south as Texas into Mexico. In Wisconsin, it can be found in a small range in the south-central and western region of the state.

Food: Omnivores, they eat earthworms, berries, beetles, grasses and other plants, and carrion (dead animals).

Mating: Late spring to early summer

Nest: Shallow, flask- shaped burrow built in loose material (dirt, soil, sandy clay)

Eggs: 2–8 eggs

Young: Hatchlings hatch 75–90 days after eggs are laid and will reach reproductive maturity at around 5 years for males and 8 years for females.

Predators: Crows, ravens, hawks, owls, raccoons, cats, foxes, and snakes

Ornate box turtles have sharp beaks, thick limbs, and a flattened dome-shaped carapace (top of shell). The carapace is brownish to black and has a starburst-like pattern on it. The skin is grayish brown with orange-to-yellow spots. They have a yellow or pale-greenish chin. Males have red-hued legs and a large inner claw. Males also have reddish eyes, while females have brown. Males are usually smaller than females.

Did you know?

The snapping turtle's sex is determined by the temperature of the nest! Nest temperatures that are 67–68 degrees produce females, temperatures in the range between 70 and 72 degrees produce both males and females, and nests that are 73–75 degrees will usually produce all males.

Most Active

Snapping Turtle, Common

Chelydra serpentina

Size: 8–16 inches long; weighs 10–35 pounds

Habitat: Rivers, marshes, and lakes; can be found in areas that have brackish water (freshwater and saltwater mixture)

Range: They are found throughout Wisconsin; also found in the eastern US and southern Canada.

Food: These omnivores (eaters of both plants and animals) eat frogs, reptiles, snakes, birds, small mammals, and plants.

Mating: April to November are the breeding months; lays eggs during June and July.

Nest: Females dig a hole in sandy soil and lay the eggs into it.

Eggs: 25–42 eggs, sometimes as many as 80 or more

Young: Like sea turtles, snapping turtles have temperature-dependent sex determination (TSD), meaning the temperature of the nest determines the sex of the young. Hatchlings leave the nest between August and October. In the North, turtles mature at around 15–20 years, while southern turtles mature around 12 years old.

Predators: Raccoons, skunks, crows, dogs, and humans

The snapping turtle's carapace (top shell) is dark green to brown and usually covered in algae or moss. The plastron (bottom shell) is smaller than the carapace. They are crepuscular animals that are mostly active during the dawn and dusk hours. Young turtles will actively look for food. As adults, they rely heavily on ambushing to hunt; they bury themselves in the sand with just the tip of their nose and eyes showing.

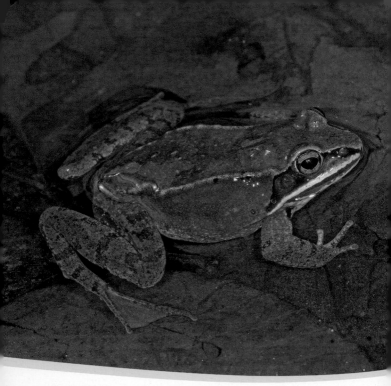

Did you know?

Wood frogs are one of the few amphibians found in the Arctic Circle. They can stop their hearts and breathing when hibernating. They have a special antifreeze that keeps their cells from freezing. Eggs are not harmed by freezing; the eggs that are fertilized will stop developing until the weather warms up.

Most Active   Hibernates

Wood Frog

Lithobates sylvaticus

Size: 2–3¼ inches long; weighs ¼ ounce

Habitat: Bogs, meadows, temporary wetlands, forests, marshes, and swamps

Range: Can be found throughout the United States as far north as Alaska and as far south as Alabama, with range extending westward into Idaho. In Wisconsin, they can be found throughout the sate minus a pocket in the southwestern region of the state.

Food: As adults: insects, snails, worms, slugs, and spiders and other arachnids. As tadpoles: vegetation, algae, and decaying plant material

Mating: Early spring in March, sometimes even before ice and snow has started to melt

Nest: No nest; lays eggs in ponds

Eggs: A mass of 1,000–3,000 eggs

Young: Tadpoles hatch 9–30 days after laying. Will turn into frogs in 6–9 weeks and reach reproductive maturity around 1–2 years.

Predators: Snapping turtles, salamanders, raccoons, skunks, beetles, coyotes, foxes, other wood frogs, and birds

Both males and females are brown, dirty red, or tannish in color. They have bumpy skin and a black mask like raccoons or superheroes! They have a pale stomach that is usually yellow to off-white. They have a skin fold that runs down the back from the eyes.

Glossary

Adaptation—An animal's physical (outward) or behavioral (inward) adjustment to changes in the environment.

Amphibian—A small animal with a backbone, has moist skin, and lacks scales. Most amphibians start out as an egg, live at least part of their life in water, and finish life as a land dweller.

Biome—A part or region of Earth that has a particular type of climate and animals and plants that adapted to live in the area.

Bird—A group of animals that all have two legs and feet, a beak, feathers, and wings; while not all birds fly, all birds lay eggs.

Brood—A group of young birds that hatch at the same time and with the same mother.

Carnivore—An animal that primarily eats other animals.

Clutch—The number of eggs an animal lays during one nesting period; an animal can lay more than one clutch each season.

Crepuscular—The hours before sunset or just after sunrise; some animals have adapted to be most active during these low-light times.

Diurnal—During the day; many animals are most active during the daytime.

Ecosystem—A group of animals and plants that interact with each other and the physical area that they live in.

Evolution—A process of change in a species or a group of animals that are all the same kind; evolution happens over several generations or in a group of animals living around the same time; evolution happens through adaptation, or physical and biological changes to better fit the environment over time.

Fledgling—A baby bird that has developed flight feathers and has left the nest.

Gestation—The length of time a developing animal is carried in its mother's womb.

Herbivore—An animal that primarily eats plants.

Hibernate—A survival strategy or process where animals "slow down" and go into a long period of reduced activity to survive winter or seasonal changes; during hibernation, activities like feeding, breathing, and converting food to energy all stop.

Insectivore—An animal whose diet consists of insects.

Incubate—When a bird warms eggs by sitting on them.

Invasive—A nonnative animal that outcompetes native animals in a particular area, harming the environment.

Mammal—An air-breathing, warm-blooded, fur- or hair-covered animal with a backbone. All mammals produce milk and usually give birth to live young.

Migration—When animals move from one area to another. Migration usually occurs seasonally, but it can also happen due to biological processes, such as breeding.

Molt—When animals shed or drop their skin, feathers, or shell.

Nocturnal—At night; many animals are most active at night.

Piscivore—An animal that eats mainly fish.

Predator—An animal that hunts (and eats) other animals.

Raptor—A group of birds that all have a curved beak and sharp talons; they hunt or feed on other animals. Also known as a bird of prey.

Reptile—An egg-laying, air-breathing, cold-blooded animal that has a backbone and skin made of scales, which crawls on its belly or uses stubby legs to get around.

Scat—The waste product that animals release from their bodies; another word for it is poop or droppings.

Talon—The claw on the feet seen on raptors and birds of prey.

Torpor—A form of hibernation in which an animal slows down its breathing and heart rate; torpor ranges from a few hours at a time to a whole day; torpor does not involve a deep sleep.

Checklist

Mammals

- ☐ American Badger
- ☐ American Beaver
- ☐ Black Bear
- ☐ Bobcat
- ☐ Coyote
- ☐ Eastern Cottontail
- ☐ Eastern Fox Squirrel
- ☐ Elk
- ☐ Fisher
- ☐ Gray Wolf
- ☐ Little Brown Bat
- ☐ Meadow Vole
- ☐ Mink
- ☐ Moose
- ☐ North American Porcupine
- ☐ Northern Raccoon
- ☐ Northern River Otter
- ☐ Red Fox
- ☐ Snowshoe Hare
- ☐ Southern Flying Squirrel
- ☐ Striped Skunk
- ☐ Virginia Opossum
- ☐ White-tailed Deer

Birds

- ☐ American Goldfinch
- ☐ American Robin
- ☐ Bald Eagle
- ☐ Barred Owl
- ☐ Belted Kingfisher
- ☐ Black-capped Chickadee
- ☐ Blue Jay
- ☐ Canada Goose
- ☐ Common Loon
- ☐ Eastern Bluebird
- ☐ Great Blue Heron
- ☐ Great Horned Owl
- ☐ Hairy/Downy Woodpecker
- ☐ Hooded Merganser
- ☐ Mallard
- ☐ Mourning Dove
- ☐ Northern Cardinal
- ☐ Northern Shoveler
- ☐ Osprey
- ☐ Red-tailed Hawk/ Red-shouldered Hawk
- ☐ Red-winged Blackbird
- ☐ Red-billed Gull

- [ ] Rose-breasted Grosbeak
- [ ] Snow Goose
- [ ] Snowy Owl
- [ ] Trumpeter Swan
- [ ] Whooping Crane
- [ ] Wild Turkey
- [ ] Wood Duck

Reptiles and Amphibians

- [ ] American Toad
- [ ] Eastern Garter Snake
- [ ] Eastern Hognose Snake
- [ ] Eastern Massasauga Rattlesnake
- [ ] Eastern Newt
- [ ] Eastern Tiger Salamander
- [ ] Gray Tree Frog
- [ ] Northern Leopard Frog
- [ ] Ornate Box Turtle
- [ ] Snapping Turtle, Common
- [ ] Wood Frog

The Art of Conservation®

Featuring two signature programs, The Songbird Art Contest™ and The Fish Art Contest®, the Art of Conservation programs celebrate the arts as a cornerstone to conservation. To enter, youth artists create an original hand-drawn illustration and written essay, story, or poem synthesizing what they have learned. The contests are FREE and open to students in K-12. For program updates, rules, guidelines, and entry forms, visit: www.TheArtofConservation.org.

The Fish Art Contest® introduces youth to the wonders of fish, the joy of fishing, and the importance of aquatic conservation. The Fish Art Contest uses art, science, and creative writing to foster connections to the outdoors and inspire the next generation of stewards. Participants are encouraged to use the Fish On! lesson plan, then submit an original, handmade piece of artwork to compete for prizes and international recognition.

The Songbird Art Contest® explores the wonders and species diversity of North American songbirds. Raising awareness and educating the public on bird conservation, the Songbird program builds stewardship, encourages outdoors participation, and promotes the discovery of nature as close as anyone's backyard.

Photo Credits

Stewart Ragan: 144

Silhouettes and tracks by Anthony Hertzel unless otherwise noted.
s=silhouette, t=animal track(s)

This image is used under Attribution 2.0 Generic (CC BY 2.0) license, which can be found at https://creativecommons.org/licenses/by/2.0/: **Judy Gallagher:** 136, original image at https://www.flickr.com/photos/52450054@N04/52292746501/

All images used under license from Shutterstock.com:

ace03: footer burst; **Robert Adami:** 86; **Tristan Adler:** 38; **Airin.dizain:** 42s; **Muhammad Alfatih 05:** 18s; **Alpha C_:** 24s, 30s, 40s, 52s; **Jody Ann:** 14; **Anthony Smith Images:** 111; **Lukasz Antoniszyn:** 37; **Victor Arita:** 19; **Agnieszka Bacal:** 35, 50; **Raul Baena:** 59; **Bonnie Taylor Barry:** 90; **basel101658:** 36s; **Clara Bastian:** 8 (state nickname); **Michael Benard:** 125; **Gabbie Berry:** 124; **BGSmith:** 16; **Karel Bock:** 131; **Todd Boland:** 113; **Miles Boyer:** 116; **Larry Burk:** 129; **Mark Byer:** 39; **Steve Byland:** 69, 77; **Mark Castiglia:** 17; **Phoo Chan:** 104; **Mircea Costina:** 56, 119; **Jim Cumming:** 30; **Ingrid Curry:** 132; **Gerald A. DeBoer:** 55; **Danita Delimont:** 24, 103; **DarAnna:** 87; **DnDavis:** 81; **Rusty Dodson:** 54; **Dominate Studio:** 14s; **dramaj:** 32s; **Ian Duffield:** 96; **Eroshka:** 54s; **FedBul:** 8 (muskellunge); **Joe Ferrer:** 110; **Deborah Ferrin:** 21; **Frank Fichtmueller:** 15; **FloridaStock:** 62; **FotoRequest:** 58, 64, 83; **Lev Frid:** 34; **Gallinago_media:** 46s; **Petr Ganaj:** 8 (wood violet); **Colin Gillette:** 128; **Bildagentur Zoonar GmbII:** 53; **gorosan:** 8 (trilobite); **Greens and Blues:** 106; **Amanda Guercio:** 120; **HannaTor:** 105; **Harry Collins Photography:** 67, 114; **Elliotte Rusty Harold:** 4; **Ayman Haykal:** 6; **Ray Hennessy:** 75; **Chris Hill:** 80; **Karen Hogan:** 82; **Intothewild_by:** 36; **Malachi Ives:** 65; **Matt Jeppson:** 127; **Vladislav T. Jirousek:** 122; **Joseph Scott Photography:** 79; **Paul Jones Jr:** 72; **Pavel K:** 12t; **Tory Kallman:** 18, 112; **David Kalosson:** 46; **Viktoria Karpunina:** 48s; **Cathy Keifer:** 70; **Keneva Photography:** 84; **Janet M Kessler:** 60; **Krumpelman Photography:** 85, 98; **Piotr Krzeslak:** 93; **Geoffrey Kuchera:** 28, 32, 52; **Holly Kuchera:** 31; **Brian E. Kushner:** 51; **Brian Lasenby:** 66, 74, 134; **Dennis Laughlin:** 12; **L-N:** 43; **Bruce MacQueen:** 71; **mamita:** 20s; **Don Mammoser:** 97, 108; **Martha Marks:** 133; **Karl R. Martin:** 78; **Kazakova Maryla:** 11 (ground nest); **David McMillan:** 8 (American robin); **Martin Mecnarowski:** 95; **Alyssa Metro:** 130; **meunierd:** 29; **Jesus_Miguel:** 94; **Elly Miller:** 63; **Miloje:** background/inset burst; **Matthieu Moingt:** 88; **MurzillA:** 38s; **Nagel Photography:** 109; **natmac stock:** 137; **Jim Nelson:** 100, 101; **nialat:** 45; **Jay Ondreicka:** 121, 126; **Paul Reeves Photography:** 42, 117; **Bill Peaslee:** 8 (American badger); **Rita Petcu:** 41; **pichayasri:** 11 (platform nest), 11 (suitcase); **Rachel Portwood:** 22; **predragilievski:** 26s; **Daniel Prudek:** 8 (honeybee); **Rabbitti:** 23, 76; **Tom Reichner:** 40, 49; **Leena Robinson:** 25; **Ron Rowan Photography:** 102; **Jason Patrick Ross:** 118; **RRichard29:** 48; **RT Images:** 107; **Ryguyryguy74:** 13; **Menno Schaefer:** 47; **George Schmiesing:** 99; **Kyle Selcer:** 8 (sugar maple); **Shoriful_is:** 91; **Benjamin Simeneta:** 135; **SofiaV:** 11 (cavity nest); **sreewing:** 26t; **Rostislav Stach:** 26, 27; **Harold Stiver:** 89; **stopkin:** 16s; **Julia Sudnitskaya:** 8 (cranberries); **Marek R. Swadzba:** 73; **Paul Tessier:** 57; **T_Dub0v:** 11 (cup nest); **Thomas Torget:** 20; **vectoric:** basketball; **Liz Weber:** 33; **w e s o m e 24:** 22s; **Mike Wilhelm:** 123; **Brian Woolman:** 92; **ya_mayka:** 44s; **yvontrep:** 68; **Alexander Zavadsky:** 8 (state motto/seal); **Oral Zirek:** 115

About the Author

Alex Troutman is a wildlife biologist, birder, nature enthusiast, and science communicator from Austell, Georgia. He has a passion for sharing the wonders of nature and introducing the younger generation to the outdoors. He holds both a bachelor's degree and a master's degree in biology from Georgia Southern University (the Real GSU), with a focus in conservation. Because he knows what it feels like to not see individuals who look like you (or come from a similar background) doing the things you enjoy or working in the career that you aspire to be in, Alex makes a point not only to be that representation for the younger generation, but also to make sure that kids have exposure to the careers they are interested in and the diverse scientists working in those careers.

Alex is the co-organizer of several Black in X weeks, including Black Birders Week, Black Mammologists Week, and Black in Marine Science Week. This movement encourages diversity in nature, the celebration of Black individual scientists, awareness of Black nature enthusiasts, and diversity in STEAM fields.

ABOUT ADVENTUREKEEN

We are an independent nature and outdoor activity publisher. Our founding dates back more than 40 years, guided then and now by our love of being in the woods and on the water, by our passion for reading and books, and by the sense of wonder and discovery made possible by spending time recreating outdoors in beautiful places. It is our mission to share that wonder and fun with our readers, especially with those who haven't yet experienced all the physical and mental health benefits that nature and outdoor activity can bring. #bewellbeoutdoors